Why
Literature
Is Bad
for You

Why Literature Is Bad for You

Peter Thorpe

Nelson-Hall nh Chicago

To: Ann and Paul

Library of Congress Cataloging in Publication Data

Thorpe, Peter.
  Why literature is bad for you.

  Includes index.
  1. Literature and morals. I. Title.
PN49.T45   801'.3   79-19092
ISBN 0-88229-486-5 (cloth)
ISBN 0-88229-745-7 (paper)

Manufactured in the United States of America

10   9   8   7   6   5   4   3   2   1

Contents

Preface

"Have Ph.D., will travel." That could have been my motto for most of my career as a professor. I've taught English at three universities, one state college, and one junior college. I traveled far and wide in Academe and enjoyed my work too, but what I ended up with was a deep skepticism about the "humanities." I'm going to put that term in quotation marks throughout this book, because I've come to suspect that the "humanities" have more to do with inhumanity than with being humane.

I'm going to try to show that too often people who spend their careers studying and teaching literature turn into something that isn't very desirable. My point is that art can be bad for us. Because I'm an English professor, I will draw most of my examples from literature, though much of what I say could apply just as well to the other arts. In the sketches and essays that make up this volume, I mention a great many literary works of the Western World. However, I keep coming back to certain touchstones—poems, plays, novels, and other prose pieces—that have a special impact on anyone in the "profession" of teaching literature. I'm thinking of standard ancient and modern epics like *The Odyssey, The Divine Comedy, Beowulf,* and *Paradise Lost;* shorter poems like *To His Coy Mistress, Elegy Written in a Country Churchyard,* and *The Second Coming;* plays like *Oedipus Rex, Hamlet,* and *The Way of the World;* novels like *Tom Jones, The Scarlet Letter,* and *Madame Bovary;* prose pieces like the King James Bible and essays by Montaigne, Johnson, Emerson, and Thoreau.

I've taught all of these many times; it would be hard to find an experienced English professor who hasn't. These are the standard classroom texts, the classics around which we in the profession center a large part of our lives. For years I believed that if a person lived with great books he would be a better specimen of humanity—more mature, aware, happy, tolerant, kind, and honest. But I'm not a believer anymore.

The idea that art can be bad for people is not a new one, nor is it the monopoly of puritans who favor censorship, oppose church music, and want to close the theatres. A number of sophisticated philosophers have told us that art corrupts us—starting with Plato, who excludes poets from his *Republic* on the grounds that they stir up our passions and distort reality. Pascal in *Pensées* attacks the theatre, because he thinks it causes the spectator's conscience to stop functioning. In *Discourse on the Sciences and the Arts* Rousseau claims the arts have a way of spreading flowers over the chains that bind people, smothering their desire for liberty. Even the liberal and tolerant Kant, in *Critique of Esthetic Judgement*, observes that art lovers don't always behave themselves:

> *virtuosi* in matters of taste, being not alone often, but one might say as a general rule, vain, capricious, and addicted to injurious passions, could perhaps more rarely than others lay claim to any pre-eminent attachment to moral principles.

And a generation ago Herbert Marcuse published *The Affirmative Character of Culture*, in which he argues that culture and the arts have the effect of relaxing our vigilance against injustice and outrage.

No, it's not a new idea. The only thing that's new in this book is the effort to go a little deeper into some of the ways in which art corrupts those who get too close to it. But this isn't a deep book. I've tried to keep from being highbrow or technical, and I've used incidents and narratives to help my concepts stick in the reader's mind.

My ideas are based on two major assumptions. One is that art doesn't exist as a thing in and for itself but rather is a large part of our environment and, as such, has far-reaching effects on us. The second major assumption is that art is essentially a means of *approval*. In recent years it has seemed to me that the act of lavishing technique and eloquence on any topic is an act of approval, because the mesmerizing brilliance with which an art classic is executed has the effect of making the content of that classic a legitimate and comfortable part of our experience, something that has gone down so smoothly that we are scarcely aware of whatever repugnance it might have had originally. Sophocles' *Oedipus Rex*, Cellini's *Perseus with the Head of the Medusa*, Goya's *The Third of May*, and Eliot's *Wasteland* are full of ugly and frightening images, yet few would deny their great beauty, and few are seriously disturbed by their content, though many would turn away in horror and disgust from the actual sight of a real man blinding himself, a warrior holding a severed head with snake-hair, innocent people being shot down, or an old man with "wrinkled dugs."

Art is usually viewed, and taught, as something that's broad, deep, and flexible, packed with the variety of life itself. But there is more propaganda than truth in this. I think it would be more accurate to say that art is a rather narrow kind of phenomenon, capable of doing only a few things over and over. One of these things is approval of its subject, regardless of what it is and regardless of what the artist may have intended. Even a satirist is prohibited by the nature of art from taking a stance against the things he purports to attack, because his artistry always makes his target too natural, too interesting and attractive. We can see this in Juvenal's *Third Satire*, a lengthy attack on ancient Rome, in which that decadent city is described with such detail that we'd all like to go there. The angry Juvenal well illustrates the principle that it's hard for art to be against anything. Genuine art is simply too good to repel us. It is an affirmation, often a joyous one, of practically everything that exists, whether it be good or evil. But ninety percent of art is about evil, for that's the most interesting thing to write about—the universe being cruel to people and people being cruel to each other and to themselves.

Art is a limited kind of thing, even though it's heresy to say it. A sure way to get a bad grade in a literature class is to argue this heresy to the professor. It isn't allowed, any more than it's allowable in Academe to say that literature and the other arts are bad for people. It's interesting to note that of all majors on the campus, only the "humanities" have an a priori set of assumptions about the supposed healthy effects of their subject matter. In other fields, we are told only that the *study* of the subject is good for us, not necessarily the subject itself. Sociology, not society; history, not war or politics; medicine, not disease; geology, not rocks. But students majoring in English can't say to someone that they're majoring in "Englishology." The subject and the studying of it have been fused so as to preclude any objective questioning about the value or actual effects of the subject.

Several years ago I heard an eminent English professor give a speech attacking a retired millionaire industrialist who wanted to endow a professorial chair dedicated to "The Fight Against Communism." The professor correctly argued that an endowment based on a preconceived thesis would go against the very purpose of the university, which was the free and open pursuit of truth, whatever that truth might turn out to be. Nobody stopped to consider that the discipline of the "humanities" also went forward on a preconceived thesis—that art is good for people. Perhaps we were too busy dragging reluctant science majors and engineers into our classrooms to "broaden" them by force-feeding them with famous works of art. We felt it was our responsibility to "humanize" these "rigid technicians" before they got out into the world where they could damage civilization with their weapons and pollutants. Now, years later, as I look back on it I feel that we not only failed to humanize them but actually succeeded in making them more inflexible and insensitive than they might have been before they were sent up to us. I feel that in those required courses we gave them enough exposure to the corrupting powers of art to make them more narrow, immature, and dishonest than they might have been before. We called this "awareness" and told them they couldn't achieve dignity without it.

I think we should continue to teach the arts but to do it in a more realistic and objective manner. Instead of starting with the old assumption that art is going to enlighten and humanize us, let's begin with a set of sharp questions about the actual effects that painting, sculpture, music, and literature have on people. Let's begin by looking for our evidence in the logical place: in the behavior of persons who commit large portions of their lives to the study of art—esthetes, critics, students in the "humanities," and above all professors who, day in and day out, live in a very close relationship with the majesty of the great classics. Let us talk about what these people are actually like and how, to the best of our knowledge, they got that way. And if, at the end of our studies, we find that art is indeed bad for us, let us study it all the more deeply and intensely, in order to learn how it corrupts us and why we always seek it out, even though we know we're going to get hurt by it.

To stop teaching literature and the other arts on the grounds that they're bad for us would be like refusing to study diseases because they're bad for us. However, maybe there should be a moratorium on requiring those who don't really want to, to take courses in the "humanities." We first have to figure out where we are. Then if we decide that every college student should be exposed to the "humanities," let us also insist that every one of them be exposed to the sciences, social sciences, and technologies as well. It is a scandal that today in most colleges a person can't get through without a dose of art but can go all the way to a doctorate, as I did, without once having been exposed to such heterodox disciplines as chemistry, physics, economics, accounting, journalism, engineering, and anatomy. C. P. Snow's *The Two Cultures and the Scientific Revolution* angered many of us in the "humanities" by pointing to our militant ignorance of science. We knew he was right, but our stubborn pride kept us from doing anything about it. I think our attitude derived from our overexposure to the arts.

Perhaps one consolation in being under the influence of the great books* is that I've had some company. I tell about them in the various sketches and essays that follow. Not that these are real people. I'd like to emphasize now that except where real names are used, the characters in this volume are fictitious, and any resemblance to persons living or dead is a coincidence. My purpose has been to fictionalize things in order to dramatize my ideas. Most of the characters in these pages are distilled essences, drawn from many observations during my travels through Academe. As such, each of them represents my efforts to be realistic. If they sometimes seem more like caricatures than characters, this is to suggest that people who spend too much time around the great books frequently end up behaving like caricatures rather than real folk. Though one can find people acting like caricatures in all walks of life, they are especially plentiful in Academe, particularly in the "humanities."

Most of us in the "humanities" lead rather unhappy lives, just as most of the artists who created the great books led unhappy lives. Indeed, for every measurable good that literature and the other arts have done people, we can find six or seven proofs of the bad effects of art, ranging from the deprivations suffered by the artist and his loved ones to the miseries experienced by generations of students forced to study his works.

Art so frequently serves its custodians as a justification for being nasty or cruel to people that it raises some serious questions about priorities, about ends and means. Sometimes I think of a possible analogy between the literary world and that of the Mafia. I used to believe that murder was merely a byproduct of the Mafia's striving for the goal of successful organized crime. Then one day, after reading Mario Puzo's *The Godfather,* it occurred to me that maybe it was the other way around: maybe the collective unconscious of the gangsters set the whole thing up so that they could more easily avail themselves of reasons to commit murder. It may be true that there is more aggression and anger in the world than there are things to be angry about, and perhaps art caters to this truth. Too many times in the world of higher learning I've seen English teachers, including myself, commit professional and pedagogical cruelties in the name of the great books. Literature was so important, we told ourselves, that it was sometimes necessary to get a bit mean or belligerent in order to keep it from being misrepresented or dragged through the dirt. There was a good feeling in my stomach when with harsh words and grades I had successfully prevented some inept student from tarnishing Shakespeare or some other great artist. It was my unfortunate duty to have to flunk the

---

*Throughout this volume I'm using the term "great books" to mean classic works of English, American, and Continental literature.

bad ones out, and I loved every minute of it. Literature was my Cosa Nostra, my vast and abiding excuse to be a higher-learning hitman and feel right about it.

So I probably don't need to go through the motions of confessing that I'm guilty of most of the sins described in this book. I hope you'll believe me when I say I'm not putting myself on a pedestal and piously pointing the moral finger at all my colleagues, past and present, with a smug holier-than-thouism. I simply want to come to you as a slightly jaded English teacher who found himself in a dark forest in the middle of his career and now thinks he sees a way out through looking at literary art from a rather negative point of view.

My approach is to look at art in terms of what I see as its actual effects on those who devote their careers to it. My conclusions are these: That literary art, instead of making us more mature, has a subtle way of guiding us into a new immaturity. That the great books, instead of endowing us with more awareness of the cosmos and the human condition, put the blinders on. That instead of showing us the way to happiness, literature moves us toward gloom. That it fogs our minds, instead of enabling us to think more clearly. And finally, that instead of improving our ability to communicate, it keeps us from getting through to each other.

The evil that literary art can do is compounded by the subtlety of artistic language. A well-written novel, poem, or play has a way of giving us the illusion that we're making intellectual, spiritual, and emotional progress rather than giving us the real thing. We feel as though we've really gotten someplace when in fact we've either stood still or slipped back. It may have been this false sense of achievement and well-being that caused Thomas Gaisford, Regis Professor of Greek at Oxford in the early 1800s, to say of a classical education, "It enables us to look down with contempt on those who have not shared its advantages." We wouldn't say this now, but many of us in the "humanities" still act it out. It's as though we've been brainwashed; in a good many of our actions we demonstrate the principle that the menace is not the acknowledged stupid person but rather the stupid person who thinks he's smart.

Deep in the basic nature of art there seems to be a force which in its effects is manipulative and conspiring. To investigate and understand this force is to begin to see how the "humanities" dehumanize. It is to begin to see a certain naiveté in William Arrowsmith's amazement that:

the wardens of Buchenwald and Belsen loved their Mozart and Beethoven, read their Goethe and Schiller. The liberal arts do not humanize unless learning finds integration in action and conduct. (*Center Magazine*, March-April, 1970)

In turning Arrowsmith's thesis upside down, I don't mean to imply that the arts can make a bad man out of a good man with wrist-flicking ease. But they can encourage certain undesirable tendencies that we already have. We're not the wardens of Buchenwald, but neither do we keep the keys to the Celestial City.

Part I

Seven
Types
of
Immaturity

Section 1

Growing Down with the Victorian Novel: The Transformation of Barbara Tieterman

*Here and there is born a Saint Theresa, foundress of nothing,
whose loving heart-beats and sobs after an unattained
goodness tremble off and are dispersed among hindrances,
instead of centering in some long-recognisable deed.*
—*George Eliot*, Middlemarch *("Prelude")*

As soon as Barbara Tieterman set foot on the university campus, she was pursued by a gaggle of young men. She dined, danced, and slept with several of them and finally settled on an intelligent football quarterback for a husband. He was a big jolly fellow majoring in accounting. He had a good sense of humor and was not unfriendly to the "humanities." By the end of her sophomore year they were married. That summer he graduated and took a job with a large firm downtown. They lived in a small apartment near the campus so that Barbara could continue her studies.

She was majoring in English, and if you had asked her, when she was a freshman, why she chose this major, she would have told you that she wanted to be "well rounded." She had gotten this from her advisor, and at the time she saw no reason to question it. But if at the beginning of her junior year you had asked her why she chose English, she would have begun her answer by muttering about the "Establishment" and how the "Now Generation" needed to "keep its goddamned eyes open to avoid being intellectually polluted." About this time, Barbara quit wearing skirts and dresses and put on Levis and a sweat shirt with a picture of

2

Bach stenciled across the front of it. She let her blond hair down, natural and wild, and began to smoke pot at the parties given by the graduate students. Her language became more colorful, and the use of "shit" became as natural to her as "geez" had been earlier. She was reading heavily now, and she began to wear glasses, the wire-rimmed granny type.

During the first year of her emancipation she liked Sartre and Camus, and took regular workouts in Hesse, Kesey, Burroughs, and Vonnegut. She read the standard English authors more as a duty than as a pleasure, though in her senior year she began to develop an interest in the Victorian novelists. The hypocrisy of the middle classes in nineteenth-century England seemed to fascinate her. During beer sessions at the grubby tavern frequented by "humanities" students, Barbara began to hold forth on Victorian Hypocrisy. She seemed to take gleeful pleasure in pointing out that the supposedly straightlaced nineteenth century had produced more pornography than any other era in English history. And she could very easily work herself into a rage by getting onto the Industrial Revolution and the way the laborers had to work and live while the industrial tycoons sat on their asses in their mansions and seduced their maidservants, kicking them out in the cold after they'd knocked them up. The Victorian period fascinated her, and the more infuriated she became, the more she studied the Victorians. It got to the point where no one, not even her professors, could argue with her about the nineteenth century. A combination of fervor and extremely heavy reading made her invincible. In class discussion, her words became so brilliant and penetrating that her classmates as they listened to her could actually forget that she was a beautiful young woman. By this time she was earning straight A's and was president of the Undergraduate English Club. She had published an essay, a reworking of one of her term papers, in a respectable journal—a fabulous feat for an undergraduate. Her professors were urging her to go on to graduate school, and there was talk about lavish and prestigious scholarships.

What was her husband doing all this time? Because he was bright he became a Certified Public Accountant a short time after graduation. He was still with the same firm, but he had moved up. He tried to interest Barbara in buying a four-bedroom house in a nice area west of town, but she wanted to stay in the apartment, close to the campus, on which she now spent upwards of twelve hours a day, usually stopping at the tavern after studying late at the library, and seldom getting home until after her husband had gone to bed. He tried to be tolerant. He knew that the great books were important to her, so he wanted her eventually to go on to graduate school. But he also wanted to start a family. He tried to talk her into taking a few years off from school for having children, but she was appalled at the idea. There was too little time, she said, too little time.

As a matter of fact, their sex life had tapered off. He didn't seem to approach her as often, and when he did, she didn't seem to want it. Moreover, she wasn't quite as attractive now. It wasn't only the sloppy clothes. She had gained weight, she didn't bathe as often as before, and she constantly smelled of sweat and incense. She didn't pick up after herself, and the little apartment was usually strewn with books and dirty ashtrays. When her husband invited his friends over, he had to do the preparatory housecleaning alone. Barbara avoided his friends and he began to see less of hers because she no longer brought them around. Things were getting pretty bad, and to patch them up he began to force himself to take more of an interest in her intellectual life. He got hold of a stack of Victorian novelists and read them doggedly each night for hours after he got home from work, though he would rather have watched television or have read *Sports Illustrated* or *Fortune*.

He tried to talk with Barbara about the novelists, but she wouldn't listen to him. She told him rather bluntly that his literary opinions were typically those of a middle-class man—simplistic and hostile to the "humanistic tradition" (as she called it). He said he couldn't help it, but the novelists he'd read struck him as destructive rather than constructive. He got a little angry and told her what he actually felt, that the Victorians appeared to him to *enjoy* telling about suffering and hatred. He had trouble understanding her belief that the novelists, by reminding us of the evil in society, could "open our goddamned eyes." Their marriage at this point came closer than ever before to breaking up.

Then she became pregnant. He was overjoyed when she told him. But she wasn't: the whole damned thing, she said, was going to mess up her first term in graduate school, which she was about to start. He tried to compromise by suggesting that she continue in school until the last month or so, and then take incompletes. They could stay in the apartment until the end of the academic year, then get a house near campus. When the child was old enough for day-care, which would be soon, she could go back to school full time. When she heard this plan, she flew into a rage. She told him that it was anti-intellectuals like him who messed up the world, who put sex and babies ahead of thinking and ideas. Then she flung out of the apartment and was gone for several weeks.

He looked frantically for her, inquired among her school friends and repeatedly asked at the tavern, but if people knew anything they weren't talking. Late one night she came back. She seemed strangely calm and looked rather pale and a bit less heavy than before. She told him that she had had an abortion. He was stunned. All he could do was stand there. She quietly told him, in the fashionable parlance of her cohorts, to fuck off. Then she gathered up some things and left. A few days later a lawyer phoned him and told him she wanted a divorce. He gave it to her. Then he quit his job and moved out to California to start over.

Barbara loved graduate school. Now she read more furiously than ever. She carried a gigantic course load and continued to get straight A's. She had a brief affair with her middle-aged Shakespeare professor, and after that she moved in with a pale young man who was trying to finish his dissertation on George Gissing, but she moved back out when it became apparent to her that she was his intellectual superior. She took up briefly with several other men, but she couldn't seem to settle down. She was infinitely busy. She literally buzzed with ideas, and she eagerly sought out discussions and arguments about anything having to do with the great books. She loved to talk, and when she wasn't carrying on about literature, she would get on the topic of her ex-husband. In her mind she had transmogrified him into some kind of monstrous infant with a fixation on the toys of the business world. How in the hell she had ever come to marry him in the first place was a real mystery. Thank God she'd finally outgrown him.

"Outgrown him." The term "outgrown" was not new. It was a cliché that Barbara had imbibed from her Shakespeare professor, who was fond of discoursing on the high divorce rate among graduate students. The explanation, according to him, was simple. Two persons get married when they are both immature and at the same intellectual level. If one of them matures and develops intellectual sophistication and the other one doesn't, somebody is going to get left behind. Usually it's the girl, the childhood sweetheart, who after faithfully supporting her husband through graduate school, gets dumped. In Barbara's case, it was the other way around. The Shakespeare professor, himself divorced, had "outgrown" his wife and had discarded her the same year he received his Ph.D. At the time he was rather sorry about it, but he knew it had to be done. As he put it, "We weren't even speaking the same language anymore. It would have been a disservice to her to string her along any longer." He had encouraged Barbara to get divorced, and when she did he was delighted.

There is every likelihood that the powers of the great books played a part in the transformation of Barbara Tieterman. She lived books, and what she read in them must have had a hand in the directions of her career and her decision to get divorced, just as excessive exposure to literature must have encouraged her Shakespeare professor to give the advice he gave her. My view is that inherent in literary art there is something that discourages people from maintaining stable relationships with others. Barbara was probably born with a streak of instability in her, but the great books took her the rest of the way. Because she was interested in the Victorian novel, it may be well to turn to this genre in our inquiry into the ways in which literature can rob us of what little stability we have. It's not too elementary a question to ask, what are Victorian novels *about*? In terms of basic plot or what happens in them, they are primarily about the destruction of family relationships.

In a sense all novelists are autobiographical. In the final analysis they can write only about themselves. This is especially observable in Dickens. Undoubtedly the worst (but in some ways the best) thing that ever happened to him was being apprenticed in a blacking warehouse when he was only nine years old. He was sent there because his father was in debtors' prison, and there was no place for young Charles to go. His stint in the warehouse was extremely humiliating to him, and it took him the rest of his life to get over it. Perhaps that is why his major works so often focus on situations in which children are orphaned or split off from their parents or loved ones, as in *David Copperfield, Bleak House, Hard Times*, and *Great Expectations*. Though it's true that he usually concludes with some kind of happy union or reunion for his heroes, the bulk of a typical Dickens novel concentrates on the *division*, not the getting together. It is displacement, not union, which really interests readers. Insofar as art is approval, Dickens is manifestly in favor of the unstable and changing relationship, for it is this and not the happy ending that receives his most sustained and eloquent artistry. Much of Dickens' power lies in the essential *homelessness* of his major works.

Many other Victorian novelists share Dickens' restlessness, though in a less showy way. Shifting, decaying, or rapidly-changing family relationships play significant parts in the plots of *Vanity Fair, Henry Esmond, The Barsetshire Novels, Wuthering Heights, Jane Eyre, Middlemarch, Silas Marner, The Ordeal of Richard Feverel, Tess of the d'Urbervilles*, and *Jude the Obscure*. These are only a few. A list of nineteenth-century English novelists who tend to concentrate artistically on unstable family relationships could easily extend itself into works of Butler, Collins,

Bulwer, Reade, Gaskell, Scott, Austen, and many others, including minor or obscure ones like Morier, Trelawny, Marryat, Galt, Ferrier, and Ainsworth. When we look into the actual lives of the novelists, we discover that many of them, like Dickens, had unhappy childhoods marked by some kind of disruption of family life. It is no overstatement to say that in a very large way, the nineteenth-century English novel is *about* the dismantling of that sacred irreducible unit, the family, without which society is in real trouble.

Whether the breakup is caused by fate, free will, or accident isn't important at the moment. What really affects us as readers is not the cause but the *fact*, the overwhelming artistic *presence* of the unstable relationship for hundreds and hundreds of well-written pages. Of course, a change in a relationship is not an evil in itself. Happiness and virtue have often resulted from offspring leaving home, marriages, making and losing friends, and even from divorces and deaths of loved ones. The evil lies in the way a good writer can reinforce and encourage any unstable tendencies we may already have, so that we become enamored of change for its own sweet sake. I suspect that an overexposure to the great books can result in a rearranging of our priorities, so that we end up in a mad perpetual search for dynamic transition, sometimes leaving human decency far behind.

The destruction of family which is so noticeable and persistent as theme and topic in the nineteenth-century English novel is really an outcropping of a deep-seated restlessness and instability that preoccupies the prose and poetry of all centuries and languages in the Western World. What seems to fascinate all writers is some kind of change in a relationship, some kind of transition from one status to another. Stasis and stability seem to bore authors; there is no conflict here, no strife or excitement to write about. Thus virtually all respectable novels, plays, and poems deal with *change*: falling in love, falling out of love, growing up, growing old, winning, losing, moving, moving, moving, in every conceivable way—physically, geographically, sociologically, spiritually. Alvin Toffler, in *Future Shock*, is right in saying that an excess of rapid and drastic change is a major problem of our time. He goes on to say that the art of today reflects this instability. I would add that art of all ages has reflected it. Future shock has been part and parcel of literature since the first poet sang. It's reasonable to assume that he who immerses himself for years in literature may begin to assimilate into his own personality an inordinate impatience with things as they are. He will continually seek change, purchasing it at a cost exorbitant to himself and to those who depend on him and love him. An apt slogan for many "humanists" would be this line from Shelley: "Nought may endure but mutability."

I return to Barbara Tieterman to think again of her lust for unstable and rapidly shifting human relationships. O where are you tonight, Barbara? Where do you wander? I heard that you got your Ph.D. (with honors, of course) and that you got an instructorship at one of the Big Ten. Was it Wisconsin? Minnesota? I heard that you had tired of the Victorians and moved into the Renaissance, after which you switched to the French Symbolistes, having gotten hooked on Mallarmé. I heard that you were doing well. You're a rather extreme case, but you make a beautiful symbol. You stand so well for mutability. You stand so well for the truth that those who live with the great books become not more grown up but more childish, more intolerant of those stable, long-term relationships which define responsible adult life. Anyone who puts art before family and friends is a child, and children are often cruel.

I think of the anecdote in Plutarch's *Life of Pericles:* "It was not said amiss by Antisthenes, when people told him that one Ismenias was an excellent piper. 'It may be so,' said he, 'but he is but a wretched human being, otherwise he would not have been such an excellent piper.'" Perhaps the same is true of those who study piping.

Section 2

How Literary Folk Thrive on Crisis

We never flinched: we sacrificed our lives
To save Greece when her whole future
Was on a razor's edge.
　　　　　　—Simonides, Cenotaph at the Isthmus,
　　　　　　　　　in The Greek Anthology

"These are the times that try men's souls." Thomas Paine wrote this famous line in December of 1776. It is the first sentence of the first of sixteen pamphlets collectively known as *The American Crisis*. The excitable Paine is in love with the word "crisis" and goes on to use it in his second sentence: "The summer soldier and the sunshine patriot will in this crisis, shrink from the service of his country." Paine's language is the rhetoric of emergency. Another one of his favorite words is "Now" (he likes to capitalize it), and he seems to thrive on situations that demand immediate and drastic action. Few men are more at home than Thomas Paine in an atmosphere of cataclysm and upheaval. He absolutely loves it. He writes excitedly, and it is a fact that his pamphlets gave a powerful boost to the morale of Washington's army.

Around 1800, after the Revolutionary era was over with and his services were no longer in demand, he fell into obscurity and eventually into a kind of disgrace. His funeral is said to have been attended by only six people, and to this day no one knows where he is buried. All we know is that he lies somewhere in his native England.

Thomas Paine was one of those men who had the misfortune to outlive his relevance and usefulness. He came when the times were ripe, but he stayed too long. Had he died in, say, 1797 (the date of his last important

9

treatise, *Agrarian Justice*), his status in literary and cultural history might have been much greater, even though it's considerable as is. Not all writers are fortunate enough to die at what seems to be the height of their powers, like Marlowe, Keats, or Dylan Thomas. What Paine needed to keep him big in the public eye were the sustained fires of crisis, but the fires died down and he disappeared into the shadows. He was miserable when he could no longer convince the public that the times were trying men's souls. The truth seems to have been that no matter what the times were like, they always tried the restless soul of Tom Paine. He was one of those persons whose very lifeblood is crisis.

What do you do if you have a disposition to thrive on crisis and there is no crisis to thrive on? Two answers come readily to mind. One is to fade away in the manner of Tom Paine. The other is to create a crisis, as William Randolph Hearst tried to do with Spain in the 1890s. Fortunately, most men don't have the power and money to do what Hearst did. However, many a man has had the genius or talent to create an imaginary crisis. Most of these men are called artists, and their imaginary crises are their works of art.

The proposition that the work of art represents a crisis can be illustrated by looking at some of the most famous works of literature of the Western World. Pluck any number out of the hat: *The Waste Land, War and Peace, Les Miserables, The Prelude, Candide, The Dunciad, Paradise Lost, Hamlet, The Divine Comedy, Beowulf,* The Gospel According to Luke, *Oedipus Rex*, and the *Iliad* and *Odyssey*. Virtually every important book in the literature of Western man derives much of its power and sense of excitement from giving the reader the impression that an emergency exists, that something must be done right away. We feel that if we don't act at once, the suitors will win Penelope, Helen will not be rescued, Thebes will fall, Christianity will be snuffed out, Grendel and his Mother will destroy Heorot, man will not reach Paradise, Denmark will rot, Paradise will be Lost, universal darkness will bury all, Pangloss' absurd philosophy will prevail, a poet's sensibility will be stifled, Jean Valjean will be identified as a convict, Napoleon will overrun Russia, and April will be "the cruellest month" on a frighteningly permanent basis.

A requirement of the artist often seems to be that to be great he must convince his audience that some sort of emergency exists. It is this sense of crisis that we retain after finishing a major classic. It doesn't matter if the emergency is rectified at the end, as in the *Iliad* and *Odyssey*. Nor does it matter that the actual, historical emergency written about was over

with long before the author wrote, as in *War and Peace* or the Gospel of
Luke. We always seem to retain that exciting sense of crisis, for it was
crisis that filled ninety percent of the book's pages.

Shorter works like lyrical poems are even more crisis-oriented. The
lyric often gets to our hearts and feelings by sustaining the emergency
through the last line. In many love poems we have a situation in which the
lover is trying to convince his mistress that if she doesn't respond *at once*
to his passion for her, he will perish or come very close to it. Because the
love lyric is usually a monologue, we seldom learn the lady's final
decision, and the poem characteristically ends on a note of crisis similar
to that with which it began. Obviously, any kind of consummative caress
would spoil the whole thing. For only on crisis can most great poets
thrive. There are exceptions, of course, like the quiet resolution at the
end of "How Do I Love Thee?" But it is fair to say that most of our major
lyric poetry is a beautiful and compelling exercise in sustained
emergency. Great literature succeeds by dint of telling us that something
has got to be done at once.

Do people believe it? Does everyone come away convinced that some
sort of emergency exists? I feel that the average reader, I mean the light,
nonacademic reader, doesn't expose himself enough to the powers of
literature to get panicky or alarmed. But what of the person who reads
heavily and seriously, and does it for a living? He is in danger, I believe,
of developing an enlarged sense of emergency, especially if he is a rather
excitable fellow in the first place. He runs the risk of becoming what I call
a "crisist," one who simply cannot stand it unless he's caught up in some
real or imaginary emergency. Usually he neither knows nor cares whether
the crisis he's struggling with is real or imagined; the only thing important
to him is that he is anxious to react. Maybe the building is on fire; maybe
he's simply paranoid; either way, the crisist feels the keen and delicious
urgency to act at once.

Now, there would be nothing wrong with crisism if it didn't harm other
people. The crisist could go his merry way and we could turn our backs
on him and plug our ears, shutting out his frantic cries for water, guns, or
demonstrations. Unfortunately, it doesn't usually work out that way. Too
often this huckster of hysteria can't leave us alone. I have seen heads roll
for the sake of his fright-peddling, as the following incident should show.

There was a young hothead in an English department at a midwestern
university who was obsessed with the problem of racism in America. Most
of his colleagues were concerned about it too, but their concern stopped

short of obsession. He seemed to resent the fact that his colleagues were merely concerned instead of obsessed; he got angry at them for not being angry. One afternoon in a department meeting, when he couldn't contain himself any longer, he leaped to his feet and gave a passionate speech in which he accused his colleagues, in a wholesale manner, of being "racist to the core."

He spoke for fifteen minutes, wildly gesticulating though not speaking loudly. His voice had the taut, quiet, hissing intensity of a man who is about to do something violent. It was a frightening and fascinating speech to hear, not only because of its vague, ominous, McCarthyistic innuendos (he named no names) but also because of its penetrating logic. Pointing out that there were no Black people in the department, either as students or as faculty, he showed that the department's admission policies and hiring practices were, paradoxically, racist even while they purported to be fair. Quite convincingly, he argued that as long as the department took in "anyone who was *qualified*," it assured itself that Blacks would be kept out. His reasoning was that because of their ghetto backgrounds, almost all Blacks would lack the qualifications to get into the department. It was a safe bet, at least at that time, that virtually no Black had a Ph.D. in English and that hardly any would have the necessary skills and high grades to become English majors at that university. The young professor concluded by telling his colleagues that by being completely "open minded," they had shut their doors on the minorities. Then he stalked out of the room. He had set off a real bomb and nobody could touch him for it, because he was right and because, of course, he had tenure (no nontenured person would have the temerity to make such a speech).

His colleagues were furious, but what could they do? Some of them talked about getting together and promulgating a denial of the charges. However, they knew that the department was at least de facto racist, if not in concept or intent. So they decided it would be better to say nothing in response to the crisist who had attacked them so viciously. But still the word rang in their ears: "Racist! Racist! Racist!"

In the meantime, the crisist's appetite for strife and upheaval had not yet been satisfied. He seemed to have gotten it into his head that somebody, a colleague perhaps, ought to pay for the damage done to the Black people. Like a ravenous wolf he began to cast his baleful eyes around the department. Within a short time he had settled on a newly hired assistant professor with a Southern drawl. It is important to mention this person's accent because that, as far as anyone has ever been able to discover, was the only piece of "evidence" that the crisist had used in coming to the conclusion that the Southerner was a racist.

In a closed meeting of tenured department members, the crisist attacked the Southerner in another fiery speech. He got results. The department chairman was easily swayed by rhetoric and the rest of the tenured staff were afraid. A secret ballot was taken, and it was decided that the Southerner should not be reappointed. As is so often the case in the academic world, he was not allowed to defend himself or even to find out the exact reasons for his dismissal. He was never officially told that the department had decided that he was a racist; he had to discover it through gossip and hallway hearsay. He couldn't fight them because they had never directly attacked him. They had played it smart, and out he went.

Though it may seem too melodramatic to mention, it needs to be said that after the Southerner was fired, his wife left him and he took to drinking a lot. It also needs to be said that to this day the department is racist on a de facto basis—almost. It has two Black graduate students. As for the crisist, he has long since forgotten his antidiscrimination campaign. Since then, he has been involved in many other crises, not a few of them of his own making.

What made him tick? I think that the perpetual crisis of literature had a strong influence upon him. Even if he had been from childhood a volatile kind of person, the emergencies of the great books probably gave him the final shove into the hasty and drastic maneuvers that sometimes terminate in the wrecking of somebody's life. I feel that the difference between the crisist and his colleagues was one of degree rather than of kind. I feel that they too thrived on emergency, though in a less flamboyant way.

I am embarrassed to admit that I have played the crisist myself in the sanctity of the classroom, when I put unnecessary pressures on the students, forcing them farther and farther into the contrived strife and hostility of intense "class discussion," the nastiness of which I used to justify on the grounds that literature was that important and that we had better act soon or civilization and culture would be drowned by the encroaching mud of middle-class mediocrity. God, was I excited in those days!

Section 3

The
Fine Art
of
Uncooperation

I am fond of the sea and all that is of the sea's kind, and fondest when it angrily contradicts me.
— *Friedrich Nietzsche*, Thus Spake Zarathustra

Quite a few of us have had the experience of driving down a major highway and coming to a place where the road swerves in order to allow for the property of someone who refused to relinquish his land to the Highway Department. I have always viewed such die-hard property owners with mixed emotions. One side of me holds them in esteem for having the courage to take a stand against the Establishment, causing tons of pavement and millions of dollars' worth of heavy equipment to go somewhere else. The other side of me feels that perhaps the Highway Department is right: there really is such a thing as progress, and it's not all bad. This side of me feels that those who impede legitimate progress are egocentrics who place their own selfishness ahead of the convenience and welfare of everyone else.

Most English professors I've met tend to favor the holdout, the person who thumbs his nose at the Establishment. I don't mean that these academicians thumb their own noses at the powers-that-be. Most of them aren't brave enough. I mean that they agree in theory, not in practice, with those who buck the status quo. However, many of them, when they can do it safely and without serious consequence, show a lack of cooperation toward sub-Establishments or social structures which have no teeth.

14

I remember one old gentleman, an American literature scholar, who almost never contributed to charities like the Heart Fund or Cancer Society. He said that charity made softies out of people and that it took more courage to withhold the money than to give it. Here he would smack his fist into his palm and quote Emerson's *Self-Reliance:* "Though I confess with shame I sometimes succumb and give the dollar, it is a wicked dollar, which by and by I shall have the manhood to withhold." Then he would say that he had outdone Emerson. Some of his students. including me, used to speculate about his "real" motivation for not contributing. Preeminent among our theories was that he was a cheapskate.

Now that I think back on it, I believe that we were wrong. I think that the mainspring of his behavior was a joy in being *uncooperative.* I am pretty sure that the old scholar had a need to indulge in difficult, contrary behavior, and that he was delighted whenever he found a safe but showy way to do it. Charitable organizations presented just such an opportunity: you could tell them to go to hell and they couldn't strike back.

I remember others who went around looking for something to refuse to cooperate with. There was one senior professor, an eighteenth-century Swiftian, who spent years trying to get on the university's athletic committee. When he finally succeeded, he never missed a meeting; and in every one of them he gave fiery speeches in which he blasted away at the "complete and utter folly" (his words) of sports and all things athletic. One time I asked him why he went to so many football games. He said he went because he was unable to restrain his savage indignation. The very thought of football, he declared, made his adrenalin surge so that he had to go to the games for a kind of catharsis. Most of us who knew him felt that without those football games he would have gone crazy. They seemed to offer the best release—or objective correlative—for his burning urge to be uncooperative. He must indeed have been in his glory when he sat there among fifty thousand fans, knowing that of all of them, he was the only one who hated football.

I would like to tell about one other. Noncooperation to this youngish gentleman, an Anglo-Saxon scholar, was a fine art. Ingenious and elaborate were his schemes for placing himself in a position to refuse to cooperate. He would go ten miles out of his way to get himself on a Ph.D. dissertation committee, if he so much as suspected that the unfortunate student's thesis might give him a chance to oppose it. And woe unto the scholar who published a book in his field! This professor could write the most vituperative, blistering (and sophomoric) book reviews ever to see print in the journals.

For a while I thought he was motivated by a sincere concern for the welfare of Anglo-Saxon studies. I thought he wrote contrary reviews only to uphold the high philological standards that were his ideal. I was disillusioned one day when he told me quite seriously that he felt rather frustrated because no one had published a book in his field for many months. At first I didn't know what to make of this statement. Later it dawned on me that he was in essence a walking bundle of unco-operativeness looking for something to be against. He didn't give a hoot about Anglo-Saxon or the whole business of scholarship. All he wanted was the excitement of ill-willed opposition. Needless to say, he never published a book himself. He was too busy practicing his philosophy of Againstism.

For a long time I disliked these three persons, the American literature man, the Swiftian, and the Anglo-Saxon scholar. I realize now that I should have checked my disliking long enough to inquire a little further into the causes of their difficult and contrary actions. Had I done so, I might have seen that one major cause was not in their personalities but in the books they had read. I think literature is a major factor in the forming of a contrary personality. Although one may have a tendency in this direction before he comes to the great books, we can wager that they will take him the rest of the way. How they do this we can discover by looking at famous novels, poems and plays.

What is it that virtually all the great heroes of literature have in common? What is it that they share, all the way from Gilgamesh to Giles Goat-Boy? Whether the heroes are epic, tragic, satirical, or comic, they characteristically are to be found in situations that pit the hero against some kind of pre-existing code, social structure, or regime whose values differ from his. The conflict (and hence the excitement and the artistry) is generated by the hero's struggle against the pre-existing world.

Any number of examples of this pattern can be seen in the traditional sort of comedy, in which a young stranger or outsider enters a social world controlled by a "narrow minded" older generation. The comic plot involves the stranger's efforts to overthrow the old social world and to form a new one of his own. At the end he is usually in control of the oldsters, the beautiful girl (often their daughter), and the money as well. Some of the best English comedies with this pattern are Congreve's *The Way of the World*, Sheridan's *School for Scandal*, and Wilde's *The Importance of*

Being Earnest. All of these plays are anticipated by the "New Comedy" writings of Menander in ancient Greece and Plautus in Rome. At the other end of our history are the comedies on television. Whether we turn to Plautus, to Congreve, or to Channel 4, we frequently come across the young comic hero in the process of overthrowing the old regime and establishing his own. We laugh with him, for the writers of comedy inevitably stack the cards in his favor, causing us to see nearly everything from his point of view and making fools out of the opposition. Things are slanted in such a manner that we usually feel that the establishment overthrown by the hero deserved to be overthrown. His uncooperativeness seems completely justified.

"Don't cooperate!"—this is the actual message or theme of most of our famous stories in the literature of the Western World, whether they are comic, tragic, ironic, or what have you. In nearly every one there is an establishment which, although it has a number of shortcomings— including perhaps a hushed-up murder—is probably no worse than the new establishment to be set up by the hero. Are we really to believe that Troy (and Helen herself) is going to be better off under the Acheans? That Canaan needs the Israelites? That the Holy Lands need the intrusion of the crusaders of chivalric romance? That Dante is better equipped to run government and Church than those he tortures in the Inferno? That Denmark would be signally less rotten with Hamlet at the helm? Or even that the academic world should make room for Jude the Obscure? If we unstack the cards and look closely at the old societies or establishments that the uncooperative heroes want to overthrow, we will find that they are not all that bad, especially in comparison with the vague and untried ideals of the hero, who so frequently is himself a hothead, an irrationalist, and above all a person who appears to thrive on conflict and strife for the sheer joy of it.

In my view radical rebellion is justified only when the opposition is truly intolerable and when it can be shown beyond a reasonable doubt that what the newcomers have to offer is going to work more than just a little better than the old way. But in so many of our great books the theme is a kind of unthinking, Yippie-oriented "do it!" Of course it can be no other way, for to have plot or action there must be strife.

Even in the tenderest love lyrics, we sense this movement to overthrow the old way. What is *To His Coy Mistress* if not a sort of linguistic conspiracy against the established and not indefensible attitudes of the lady? The same point can be made about any number of love poets who make similar pitches—from Propertius to Petrarch, from Ronsard to the present day. The approach is always the same: change your ways; discard your identity and don a new one just for me; drop everything and come running to me, even if it means throwing out everything you've worked to establish. Slightly magnified, these demands are the same as the ones made by heroes in our great epics, dramas, and novels.

If we fail to realize the absurdity of the hero's demands, we can be forgiven; for the artistry of any classic literary work is enough to disguise the slant and bias of the presentation. It is Hamlet's gorgeous complexity that causes us to stop short of seeing that the court of Claudius, though not quite honest, is really a harmonious place, probably not worth destroying merely to satisfy some individual's lust for revenge. But Shakespeare does everything he can to prevent us from seeing it that way. He makes us see the court from a much greater distance than we see Hamlet from, and he gives Hamlet the best poetry.

Great heroes in literature are great by dint of eloquently refusing to cooperate with the establishments into which they have been born or have intruded. It is reasonable to suspect that a person who spends his life reading this kind of material can develop an uncooperative attitude, whether or not there is anything to be uncooperative about.

Section 4

Fate and Determinism as Cop-Outs

Free will they one way disavow,
Another, nothing else allow.
—*Samuel Butler,* Hudibras, *Canto I*

"Self-reliance": unfortunately that expression has something hackneyed and shopworn about it. Maybe it was all right for the nineteenth century, but as modern intellectuals, we tend to feel that it's a little late for it now in our post-Freudian age, when much of human behavior can easily be explained (so we like to think) as controlled by such deterministic forces as "the unconscious," "instinct," "society," "ecology," "Skinnerism," or "brainwashing." My point is that there is still room in our modern age for self-reliance but that a number of forces, including literature, militate against it. In fact literature has always undermined our belief in freedom and the responsibility that goes with it; it's just that today several other forces, like those named above, have come to literature's aid in inculcating the idea that man is trapped and weak. So it's easier to believe it now than it was in past centuries.

It's hard to talk about freedom and responsibility without getting bogged down in philosophical arguments. It's like grabbing hold of a piece of floating seaweed and discovering that it has a thousand other pieces of seaweed attached to it. One can't take anything without taking the whole package. I got caught in the seaweed one day about a decade ago. I was jogging with a friend of mine, an attorney who has little patience with philosophical abstractions. We had finished our run, and

19

since it was a cold day we decided we'd sit for a while in the sauna bath at the university gym. We got to talking about how free or unfree a person is when he votes. Is he thinking for himself or is he simply voting as his parents did or as his friends and boss tell him? My friend claimed that all men could, if they chose, stand on their own two feet, make their own decisions, and be captains of their fate (he quoted part of Henley's *Invictus*).

I was shot full of heavy, turn-of-the-century novelists at the time, so I opted for—what else?—determinism. Ah yes, "Among the forces which sweep and play throughout the universe, untutored man is but a wisp in the wind." Baloney, said the lawyer, the novelists were a bunch of sentimentalists who couldn't bear to let man take the blame for anything. So every time they wrote, they distorted everything to show man as helpless. I was appalled at this short shrift! Hadn't Zola, Hardy, Crane, and all the others shown time and time again that man is not free? Wasn't he, the lawyer, sitting there in that hot sauna bath because the biology at work in him told him it would feel good? The lawyer retorted that he was there because he damn well chose to be.

About this time, a shadowy figure in the dark corner of that hot sauna spoke up: "Allow me to clarify your argument"—and before we could tell him to stay out of it, he began lecturing on David Hume, the eighteenth-century philosopher. Hume said that the old argument between free will and "necessity" was a waste of time because there were no premises to argue on. To believe in necessity or determinism, one has to believe in cause and effect. To the skeptical Hume, there is no such thing. He argues that when you look at experience, you see only that one thing *follows or occurs after* another thing, not that one thing *is caused by* another thing. Lightning strikes and then we hear the thunder, but there is no way in the world to prove logically that the lightning *caused* the thunder. Therefore, says Hume, it is absurd to try to argue about such causal matters as necessity.

Having destroyed that one, Hume (who was about twenty-six at the time) turns to freedom of the will. The will, he says, is of course part of the mind. The trouble is, there is no way to prove that the mind exists. When you look into yourself and try to perceive your own mind, you can perceive only fleeting ideas and impressions, not the mind itself. Ideas and impressions are merely *evidence*, not the real thing. Hume's skepticism goes to the extreme of denying the existence of that which cannot be *produced*, even though we have traces and signs of it. How foolish, then, to try to argue about the freedom of the will, when the will, as part of the mind, cannot even be proven to exist. The whole argument of determinism vs. free will was an idle and useless business. Thus the Shadowy Figure in the corner of the sauna bath concluded his lecture. We "thanked" him (we weren't sure for what) and came away, leaving him there in the 185-degree darkness.

After we got outside, the lawyer mumbled that the Hume approach was one giant cop-out—a lot of academic jargon calculated to mystify rather than clarify. I partially agreed, though I thought to myself that the Shadowy Figure had done a pretty good job of explaining Hume, whom I'd read but never understood very well. My friend and I parted, I to my class and he to his downtown office, where he was preparing to defend a man who had gone beserk and murdered his wife with a hammer. I found myself lecturing that afternoon on the way that literature, by explaining man, caused us to develop attitudes of forgiveness and understanding—*tout comprendre, c'est tout pardonner.* As I lectured, I was thinking in the back of my mind that the lawyer was too simplistic. If at that time someone had told me that I would someday side with him, I would have said that that someone was crazy.

As it turned out, I did in later years shift my philosophy toward an emphasis on free will, self-reliance and responsibility, though I stopped a little short of my friend's position. What caused my shift was my discovery that literature may be (to borrow the lawyer's term) a cop-out in the sense that it usually functions to excuse man for whatever he does. This excuse making is usually passed off as "insight" or "human understanding."

Much of the earliest literature is religion. The Bible and Greek mythology were all believed once. Like all religions, they were conceived in order to make some sense out of man's universe and to answer questions: Why does the serpent crawl on its belly? Why does man have to work? Why does he have to die? Why do women have to suffer pain in childbirth? The answers are all there in the Hebraic and Hellenistic myths. An interesting fact about answer mongering is that the answers usually have the effect of relieving man of responsibility. To explain why the serpent crawls on its belly is to go into the story of how it helped bring about the Fall. The result is that man is partially excused from his transgression and that part of the blame is shifted onto something outside of himself.

The poets, novelists and dramatists of later times are no different in that they tend to blame everything but mankind. If they are medieval writers, they like to blame the Devil or Fortune's Wheel. If they are medieval or Renaissance allegorizers, as in *Piers Plowman* or *The Faerie Queene*, they put the blame on personified abstractions like the Seven Sins or Duessa. If they are novelists, they blame psychology or the deterministic forces of the cosmos and society.

There is something inherent in the nature of literature that discourages the artist from seeing man as responsible. To write a significant book or poem is to explain. To explain is to forgive. To forgive is to excuse from blame. The poet's business is largely to objectify, and the very act of using a figure of speech or a metaphor has the effect of transferring what was inside of us to the outside, where it no longer seems part of us and where, consequently, we blame it and not ourselves. Indeed, the literal meaning of "metaphor" is "to carry beyond," which suggests something about the role of this device.

The way that metaphor can transfer responsibility away from man can be illustrated with some famous images in Shakespeare. Everyone has heard of "flaming youth," "the green-eyed monster," or "the dogs of war." In each case, an internal, abstract characteristic of mankind—his impulsiveness, his jealousy, his aggression—is transformed into a physical object (fire, monster, dog) which has separate existence from an integral human being. To talk about man in such language is not really to talk about him but rather to talk all around him, so that no matter what is said—good, bad or indifferent—it is never really said about man. The actual topic in a great many poems is not mankind but the physical and mechanical surroundings that the poet metaphorically creates for him.

It has to be this way if poetry is to be exciting or interesting, for naked abstractions like pride, greed, hostility, etc., are dull by themselves. Yet only through such abstractions can we deal accurately with human behavior; and next time someone tells us his love is like a red, red rose we'll know that such a statement sheds much more light on roses than on love. It is one of the limitations of literature that to be beautiful or powerful it has to be at least slightly vague or inaccurate. Few will deny the force and loveliness of famous expressions like "through a glass darkly," "drink to me only with thine eyes," "far from the madding crowd," or "nature red in tooth and claw." But few will step forward to tell us exactly what they mean. To be good they simply must be unclear.

Literary language, then, tends to externalize man's nature, and in the process that nature is transformed into something beyond the realm of the strictly human. I have long observed that people in the "humanities" are singularly inept and benighted when it comes to explaining, understanding, and handling human beings. I used to be embarrassed by what I thought was a discrepancy between the "insights" of art and the blindness of art followers. Now I am pretty sure that no discrepancy exists, for in a manner of speaking, art is blindness. However, what does exist is a sentimental habit among "humanists" of making excuses for everything and everybody. Because they live each day with suprahuman material, the teachers of art look for suprahuman reasons for behavior. The result is that in theory nothing is ever anybody's fault.

My own view is that men are basically free, some more so than others. I like the attitude of Thomas Reid, the next major British philosopher after Hume. Reid felt that even if we can't prove we exist or even if "necessity" prevails, we must use our "common sense" to go ahead and act *as though* we were free, and get on with the job of life. Therefore I have grown impatient with literature's persistent habit of assigning blame and responsibility to gods, personifications, society, etc.—things outside of man himself. It seems to me that if man is to survive he must at least assume that he is free. In achieving this freedom, he doesn't have to ignore his limitations. Nor does he have to listen too much to the poets. For too few writers seem to be masters of their fate.

Section 5

Turning Self-Knowledge into Self-Centeredness

The hidden well-spring of your soul must needs rise and run murmuring to the sea;
   And the treasure of your infinite depths would be revealed to your eyes.
                                        —*Kahlil Gibran*, The Prophet

I'm skeptical about psychoanalysis. I have seen a good many persons go through it, and most of them seem to come out very much the way they went in. Oh, they know more about themselves now, and they say they feel more at peace with themselves and the world, but they go right on acting the way they did before. And most psychiatrists or practicing psychologists I've seen appear to be as messed up as the patients they're supposed to be treating.

In making these jaundiced remarks about psychoanalysis, I haven't meant to deny that it can open up our souls and allow us to know more about ourselves. What I'm questioning is the necessity or wisdom of deep self-knowledge. Some self-knowledge, yes, of course. But too often we assume, without really thinking it out, that a total acquaintance with our own being is a worthy and important goal. This assumption underlies at least eighty percent of the verbiage emanating from creative writers, and perhaps ninety percent of the lectures I used to give about literature.

The major authors in English, and in many other literatures, love to give us the impression that in their works the layers of illusion are being deftly peeled away so as ultimately to lay bare the stark truths of existence—yours, mine, everybody's. The most tedious peeler, in my view, is Joseph Conrad, who loves to make us pile aboard a shaky old

24

vessel and journey up some primeval river, verbosely "penetrating" further and further into the jungle of our psyches until there, at the heart of darkness, is—well, maybe not the Secret of Life, but at least a few trembling words about the inner human horror that we average people have all failed to see.

Even when writers profess to know nothing about the inner man, they often make the profession in a way which suggests that they really know plenty. When D. H. Lawrence says (in his essay on Benjamin Franklin) "The soul of man is a dark forest," he says it with a kind of knowing Satanic smirk, so that the profession of ignorance actually becomes a species of knowledge. When I first read that ominous Lawrence sentence I was young and it was news to me that my soul was a dark forest. For several days I went around with this crushing insight on my mind, until I read some other author, who sent me off in a new direction. When I was a student it seemed as though the only thing I changed more often than my Philosophy of Life was my socks. But through all of my philosophical bypaths and crooked ways, two things consistently stayed with me: my conviction that self-knowledge was crucial and my opinion that it was to be found in the great masterpieces of English literature. Sadder and I hope wiser now, I no longer cleave to either of these views. I don't think that literature can do what psychiatry is supposed to do, and even if it could, it shouldn't.

What does literature do? I believe the infectious energies of great works of art have a way of instilling in us a drive to acquire self-knowledge, but I doubt that such a drive is a virtue, especially when art, which makes us itch with questions, gives us so few answers. Thus a common ailment among those who make a career of letters is an annoying restlessness something like the dementia praecox that we all should have outgrown long ago. But the main trouble with the excessive soul-searching that art inspires in us is not that it yields no answers but that it results in self-centeredness.

The self-centered man is defective as a human being, for he is so engaged with himself that he has little time for anyone else. I remember an English professor in his forties who read so deeply and thought so hard that he finally abandoned his wife and children. When we asked him why he did it, he said, "We destroy each other." His favorite novel was *Madame Bovary;* he was always poring over it and explaining its "wisdom" to his classes. He thought he had gotten a great amount of self-knowledge from it, but I think he had gotten only the illusion of self-knowledge. Even if Flaubert had somehow transcended the restrictions and narrow conventions which are inherent in literature, giving the reader real self-knowledge, there is no guarantee whatever that the reader would have the sense to put that self-knowledge to work so as to make himself and others better and happier.

Literature presents us with an interminable parade of famous characters who are completely hung up on themselves. Through the pages of the great books walk some of the most self-centered personalities ever conceived: Prometheus, Cleopatra, Dante, Faust, Hamlet, Clarissa, Young Werther, Childe Harold, Pip, Leopold Bloom, Willy Loman, and Holden Caulfield. The author of each of these personalities may intend to approve or disapprove, but his artistry inevitably makes each of them attractive. Their egocentricities range wide, from the exhaustive self-examinations of Job to the scatological scrutinies of Portnoy, but they all have in common a tremendous sense of their own self-importance, either consciously or unconsciously. Although, like Job, they may profess charitable motives, the manner in which the artists present them to us characteristically places their personal problems and goals ahead of everything else, even if it means the destruction of everything around them.

Authors seem to see a virtue in asserting the self over the cosmos and one's fellowmen. But seldom in the great books is the opposite thesis argued. Among our major writers there are few genuine spokesmen for the view that the path to human decency lies in negating the self so as to serve others. This of course is the way it must be, for a truly selfless and charitable hero would scarcely be able to generate the conflict on which all literature is predicated. In the majority of the famous literary works most of the author's efforts go toward dramatizing the struggle of the hero to fulfill his own goals. Even in the portrayal of seemingly selfless characters like the Vicar of Wakefield, Hester Prynne, or Billy Budd, the accent tends to fall not on their passivity but on the way in which that passivity is transformed by the natural pressures of society into a kind of "justified" aggression. Energy, action, struggle, conflict: these are what art demands. To make such a demand is rather automatically to throw the emphasis upon the asserted self, without whose assertion there can be no conflict and, hence, no art.

Literature has a number of built-in messages, one of which is that *you*, as an individual, are overwhelmingly important. Billy Budd, thrust from a life of quiet into a context of strife, is a near-relation to Captain Ahab in that both men are shown trooping their own egos against the grain of everyday life. The fact that Melville uses powerful artistry and eloquence to depict these two only makes their self-concern more attractive to us.

Even the much-talked-about "universality" of art may be an inimical force in that it too often has the effect of making things relevant to our sense of "I" and "Me," and not to mankind in general. Too often the effect of the archetypal or déjà vu element in literature is not to broaden our horizons but to shorten them, always by bringing us directly back to ourselves. To mouth the truth that art is universal is really to cater to a "what's in it for me?" approach to things.

I don't think it's any exaggeration to say that an overexposure to the great books can bring about a drastic increase in the self-centeredness that all of us are born with. The result is that we are moved even farther away from the finest and cheapest therapy of all, which is going out of ourselves and helping others.

Section 6

How Literature Gives Us the Lust for Revenge

Ghost. *Awake Revenge; for thou art ill-advised*
To sleep away what thou art warned to watch!
Revenge. *Content thyself, and do not trouble me.*
    —*Thomas Kyd*, The Spanish Tragedy, *III. xiv.*

The Merchant of Venice was the first work by Shakespeare that I read. At the time (I was in early adolescence) I thought the plot was rather interesting but got bogged down in the poetry and the thought content. I didn't get truly excited about the play until many years later when I was in graduate school, by which time I had read a great deal of Shakespeare.

One morning in the graduate-student lounge I came across a paperback edition of the play which contained an introduction by a well-known old-time Shakespeare scholar. He argued that in effect *The Merchant of Venice* was a treatise against revenge. He said that if you attacked someone, then that someone felt justified in striking back at you. Then you in turn would feel that you had the right to counterattack, which of course would encourage your opponent to counter-counterattack. Thus revenge was apt to turn into an endless chain of retaliations, benefiting neither party and injuring both. Not until someone exercised restraint or turned the other cheek could the chain be broken.

That was what *The Merchant of Venice* was all about. When Portia says, "The quality of mercy is not strained," she means that Shylock should go easy on Antonio. Even though the Jew has the legal right to collect his bond, or his pound of flesh, to do so would be to perpetuate the sad chain of revenge. The play dramatizes the truism that vengeance of any sort is a deadly folly and that the way to peace and virtue is through charity and restraint. I came away utterly convinced that the old scholar was right. What a brilliant introduction to the play!

Later that day I was in a beer tavern, shooting the breeze with several other graduate students. When the talk drifted onto Shakespeare, I had an opportunity to reveal my newly acquired insight into *The Merchant of Venice*. Most of my comrades were really impressed with it. But one of them, a fellow with a long name I've forgotten, attacked me vigorously. He said that the play was not a sermon against revenge; rather, it was primarily a "poetic study" (his words) of the Jews in England in the late sixteenth century. I countered with the view that certainly a study of revenge could coexist in the play with a study of English Jewry. The fellow retaliated by reminding me that I had originally described the play as a "treatise," not a "study." He then went on to point out that Shakespeare was a poetic dramatist, not a writer of sermons or treatises. I blasted back at him by saying that if Shakespeare was no sermonizer he was also no writer of "studies." But my opponent now trapped me by reminding me that I had just *referred* to the play as a "study." I was cornered. And now I began to see in the faces of the other students that they had abandoned me and were siding with that despicable pedant. I was defeated, and it took me a long time to live down that humiliating session at the tavern.

It took even longer—a decade, in fact—for me to discover what *The Merchant of Venice* was really about. It was neither a treatise against revenge nor a study of English Jewry in Shakespeare's time. It was, insanely, a kind of treatise in favor of revenge. The old scholar in his introduction to the play had concentrated on the noble sentiments in Portia's speech to the exclusion of nearly everything else. He had ignored the actual story: one man spits on another man and tries to wreck his business; the other man retaliates by loaning the first man money on impossible terms and then trying to collect in blood; friends of the first man get back at the money-lender by (1) getting out of the loan on a technicality and (2) stripping the money-lender of both daughter and ducats; bereft of power and influence, the money-lender is unable to strike back, and the play ends. There is no question as to who wins in this one.

Isn't it possible that such a story, told and embellished with some of the finest poetry in English, reinforces the idea that revenge can get you somewhere? Isn't it possible that what *The Merchant of Venice* really suggests is that revenge is not an endless chain but rather a valid and effective way permanently to subdue your enemies? If art is approval, Shakespeare in this influential work has taken a stance strongly in favor of one of the ugliest tendencies in human nature.

Suppose, however, that the revenge against Shylock had failed. Indeed, the play comes close to ending that way, veering dangerously toward tragedy in the famous trial scene in the fourth act. How would we have responded if Antonio had perished? The probable answer, it seems to me, is that it wouldn't have made any difference. The play's dominant material is revenge; and no matter how that material is arranged, it still receives the dazzling inimitable stamp of Shakespeare's poetry—in essence, a stamp of approval. Perhaps the chief difficulty with Shakespeare is that he writes so well that he is finally incapable of disapproving anything. His language tends to get us intoxicated with the subject, no matter what it is.

In upholding the doctrine of revenge, Shakespeare has plenty of support from other writers. He lived in an era when vengeance was a major literary theme (as in the plays of Kyd, Marston, Webster, and Tourneur), though in no age does it completely vanish from art. Thousands of poets have sung of war, of which revenge inevitably becomes a part, regardless of the original cause of the battle. War is by definition a series of retaliations. Whatever the poet's original intent, to train the guns of art on the battlefield is to worship at the shrine of Nemesis.

Such was the case with British World War I poets like Wilfred Owen, Robert Graves, Siegfried Sassoon, Edmund Blunden, Francis Ledwidge, and Rupert Brooke. They seem to represent a variety of approaches, ranging from the steely patriotism of Brooke to the elegiac vision of the horrors of war in Owen. What they all have in common, however, is a fascination with warfare, which they reveal in a number of unforgettable images like Sassoon's "ninestone corpse with nothing more to do" or Owen's "cartridges of fine zinc teeth." With strong language like this, the war is so powerfully etched into our attention that we tend to forget the point that the poet is making about it. To say that we read these poets only for their "message" and not really for the fascinating images of war is like saying we went to see *The Godfather* to learn about business ethics.

Vengeance bulks large in the literature of hatred and war, but it is also a persistent motif in the quieter or more introspective kinds of writing. It is probably not extravagant to say that there is no such thing as a literary work which lacks the potential for developing a theme of revenge. We have only to consider that all literature contains conflict and that conflict is essentially a fluctuating retaliatory struggle, in which first one side then the other dominates. When the strife ends, the poem does too. This is true not only of characters but also of ideas. In Yeats' *The Second Coming* the conflict occurs not between men but between cultural epochs or cycles of history. The poem begins with one epoch pushing the other one out of the picture, but before it is over we have received ample warning that neither epoch can endure. For Yeats, history is defined through the reciprocal and retaliatory strife of opposite cultures. It seems hard to escape the conclusion that all literature implies conflict and all conflict implies revenge.

If I've been right in saying that the theme of revenge is enticingly present in the very nature of the literary work, then we shouldn't be surprised or disillusioned when we discover that not a few of our colleagues in the "humanities" have more than a smattering of vindictiveness in their personalities. Revenge feels good, and art makes it feel even better.

Section 7

Learning to Hate the Older Generation

King. *I know thee not, old man: fall to thy prayers;*
How ill white hairs become a fool and jester.
　　　　　　　—*Shakespeare*, Henry IV, Part I, *V. v.*

A few years before the time of Christ, the ancient Roman poet Horace addressed a compliment to a fellow writer. "Fundanius," Horace wrote,

> . . . you are the only contemporary writer
> Who can capture the true style of the conversation
> Of the wily courtesan or of Davus the slave,
> In the grand manner of the New Comedy,
> As they set a trap for the old man named Chremes.

These lines, from the Tenth Satire of the First Book, suggest that the comic pattern of youngsters against oldsters was a familiar cliché even then. The chief Roman writer of New Comedy was Plautus, who lived a couple of centuries before Horace. Many of his plays are based on situations in which boy gets girl by overcoming or maneuvering around her parents or guardians. In a Plautine comedy, the young folks win and the old ones lose, and the play is essentially a celebration of the victory of youth. Like a great many ancient Romans, Plautus drew heavily on the Greeks, his chief predecessor being Menander, whose works survive only in fragments, though there is enough left to tell us that he was fascinated with the kind of plot that involves a generation gap.

If we go back farther in literary history, we come across Old Comedy, of which the most famous author is Aristophanes. A major difference

32

between Old and New Comedy is that the Old gets very personal in its satire, often naming names and sometimes even satirizing people in the audience, whereas New Comedy, which was spawned by the more restrictive government which came to power in Athens after the Golden Age, uses safer, anonymous type-characters of the sort that Horace mentions. Professors who lecture on Old and New Comedy like to stress the many differences between the two genres, sometimes overlooking a very important similarity: both deal with the generation gap.

The gap in Old Comedy is less observable because it seldom takes the form of fathers or mothers against sons or daughters. Instead, Aristophanes and his contemporaries liked to write of situations in which youthful characters were pitted not against their parents but against other kinds of senior authority figures like gods, teachers, military officers, or government officials. The idea was to make fun of authority, to bring it low by having the wanton desires and rebellious attitudes of youth triumph over it. This of course is the business of New Comedy too, though it is accomplished in a different form. But the point is that the basic material of both Old and New Comedy is youthful rebellion against elder authority. This is also the essential matter of succeeding comedies, from the times of the ancient Greeks and Romans all the way down to the present day. In terms of young against old there is no real difference between Aristophanes' *The Clouds* and *Father of the Bride*. Without the generation gap to exploit, Shakespeare, Lope de Vega, Molière, Wilde, and many others could not have achieved fame as writers of comedy. Needless to say, comedy doesn't restrict itself to the stage. When we turn to comic novels, short stories, or poems, we find that the great majority of them draw heavily on the generation gap for story and theme.

On the other side of the coin is tragedy. It also frequently exploits the generation gap, though in a different way. If in comedy the oldsters are overthrown, in tragedy they tend to win out. At the end of *Romeo and Juliet*, the youngsters have been destroyed but the parents are still alive and healthy, though their experiences have made them somewhat sadder and wiser. The same thing happens in innumerable tragedies, dramatic or non-dramatic, of all periods of literature. The exuberant spirit of youth is quelled by authority, which may manifest itself as parents, rulers, military persons, or any number of characters who have a sufficient amount of the stern inflexibility associated with age.

If in a manner of speaking comedy is successful revolt against authority, tragedy is crushed rebellion. But in either case the villains are the oldsters, or sometimes youngsters who are bad by dint of impersonating oldsters. Malvolio in *Twelfth Night* is not an old man, but his unbending puritanism makes us think of him as a father figure, the kind of person who smacks of authority, loves curfews, never smiles, and doesn't want anyone to have any fun. Because Shakespeare's play is a comedy, Malvolio is put out of the way at the end, shoved safely to the side so that the youths can go ahead with their dances, feasts and marriages. If it were a tragedy he would still be in power at the conclusion. In either case, we as readers wouldn't be caught dead siding with him.

Just as Malvolio is not literally a member of the older generation, the youthful characters in comedy and tragedy are not always young. Sir John Falstaff, who is at least sixty, acts the part of a swaggering young man who doesn't have a care in the world. At one point in the First Part of *Henry IV* he gets a laugh by saying, "They hate us youth." But there is also some truth to his pronouncement, for in many ways he is more juvenile than either Prince Hal or Hotspur. And the King, who is actually younger than Falstaff, is made to seem much older by being in a position of authority and conducting himself with an almost excessive gravity: "Uneasy lies the head that wears a crown."

The oldsters and youngsters in literature, then, sometimes identify themselves more by the roles they play than by their actual chronological ages. The fact that a dramatist can make old men into young ones or vice versa suggests not only that he is a good playwright but also that we as an audience may have certain preconceived ideas about what constitutes youth and age, ideas which the playwright can manipulate and exaggerate. Whether or not our concepts of youth and age are accurate is by and large irrelevant. The only thing that matters for the successful portrayal of older and younger generations in literature is what we can be led to believe, not what might actually be true. What most readers end up believing is that an inflexible and authoritarian attitude is to be equated with age and a liberal, lively attitude with youth.

The only major literary tradition in which age is rather consistently respectable is the epic. Nestor and Mentor in Homer, Anchises in the *Aeneid*, Hrothgar in *Beowulf*—all of these are characters who have attained wisdom and dignity with age, not the irascible inflexibility so often assigned to senior citizens in comedy or tragedy. But does it follow that epic is really sympathetic toward the older generation? I think the answer is no. Although characters like Nestor or Hrothgar are shown in a favorable light, they are not shown enough to win our sympathy. Compared to our sustained exposure to youthful heroes like Odysseus, Aeneas, or Beowulf, we see very little of the oldsters in the epics, so that even though the poet may intend us to warm to them, we are precluded from doing so because we can't spend enough time with them. Thus, even in a genre which purports to take a kindly view of age, the cards are still stacked on the side of youth.

We may add here the reflection that the virtuous oldsters both within and outside of the epic tradition tend to be rather dull. Clean old men like Squire Allworthy in *Tom Jones* or the stuffy, ultraresponsible fathers in Jane Austen are so dry and dull that we are thankful that we don't see much of them. In those rare cases in which the oldsters do become interesting, they usually do it by closely imitating the energies, dynamism, and rebelliousness of youngsters, as in *King Lear*, or as in Yeats' later poems, in which he sees himself as physically old but spiritually young and vital. In an early novel called *The Poorhouse Fair*, John Updike tried to reverse the traditional generation gap by having the aged inmates of the poorhouse play the part of exuberant rebels against the inflexible policies of their middle-aged superintendent. But Updike gave his main character, a ninety-year-old, so much energy and so many authority problems that for all practical purposes he turned him into a youth. It seems that even when authors try to side with the elderly, the basic structure of literature is such that it is virtually impossible for them to do so. It's hard to escape the conclusion that inherent in literary art there is something that rejects or opposes age.

Literature's built-in bias against age also shows up in lyrical poetry. In the world of the lyricist, one of the worst things you can say about someone is that he's old, as in Shelley's reference to George III as "An old, mad, blind, despised, and dying king." A similar attitude, by the way, can be seen in the powerful cartoons of David Levine. When he draws someone he hates—Nixon or Humphrey, for example—he makes them look very old and withered; but when he drew Stravinsky, whom he loves, he made the composer, who was several decades older than Nixon or Humphrey, look astonishingly young.

In love lyrics, the constant fear is of growing old, which for the poet spells the end of love. Many of the great Renaissance sonnets by Petrarch, Wyatt, Surrey, Sidney, Spenser, Shakespeare, and Drayton have an obsession with the "hideous prospect" of old age. Poets like these have overreacted to the natural aging process to such an extent that even forty seems ancient, as in Shakespeare's Sonnet 2, which begins with the ominous "When forty winters shall besiege thy brow." There are of course a few poets who see beauty in age, Robert Frost being one of the best. But for every Frost there seems to be a dozen lyricists who hate and fear anything over thirty like the plague itself.

It is somehow appropriate that many of the greatest love poets died young—Catullus, Propertius, Wyatt, Surrey, Lovelace, Suckling, Burns, Keats, Hart Crane, and Dylan Thomas. It's not easy to think of many epic poets who died young, for an epic is usually the undertaking of a middle-aged man who is presumably mature as well as learned. Many satirists too seem to live a long time, or at least to a ripe later middle age, as if the venom and vinegar of their kind of writing were some sort of life-sustaining force. We think of such durable lampooners as Horace, Juvenal, Dryden, Swift, Pope, Voltaire, and Twain, all of whom reached fifty at least. (The dour Orwell made it to forty-seven.) Nevertheless, a good many villains in satire are oldsters who, though they stand accused of other crimes, are also accused of the sin of being old, like Dryden's Achitophel.

In looking at the generation gap in literature of all kinds, we are repeatedly invited to embrace the thesis that in the world of the creative writer it's unforgivably bad to be old. There are exceptions, of course, but it seems safe to say that in most of the great books of the Western World, the oldsters get short shrift, whether the author intends it or not.

In view of the kinds of persons who turn to creative writing, it's really no surprise to find that literature is automatically prejudiced against age. For it often seems that in order to succeed, a literary artist has to possess the energies which derive from intense authority problems, and the lives of writers are fraught with stories of unhappy childhoods and difficulty with parents. Perhaps a playwright, novelist, or poet is a person who is by nature more rebellious than there are things to rebel against, a person who therefore finds it necessary to create fictions in which there is some stern and elderly authority to struggle against. In any case, in the fictions of the great books, the generation gap is real.

But how real is it in actual life? In these days, when we speak of the generation gap, we too often beg the question of whether such a gap exists in the first place. There may be no such thing, according to Norman Podhoretz, one of my favorite iconoclasts and a very able reverser of clichés. Editorializing in *Commentary* for August, 1970, he wrote:

I found myself consoling a friend the other day with the reflection that he and his nineteen-year-old son, with whom he had just had an unpleasant argument, enjoyed the distinction of representing one of the few true instances of the generation gap I had yet run across after years of diligent searching.

Podhoretz was writing in the context of politics, maintaining that most youngsters vote pretty much like their parents, but he also suggested that the generation gap has been vastly exaggerated in many other areas of life.

My own view is that as soon as we close our great books and take a look at the real world around us, we discover that for every difference between father and son there seem to be fifteen or twenty similarities. Indeed, sometimes it appears that the strife between generations arises precisely because the generations are so much alike. However that may be, our authors may be guilty of overstating a trivial problem, of making a mountain out of a pimple and inspiring contempt if not hatred in their readers for older people, about whom it has yet to be proved that they are any more evil than the young.

Authors are a minority among us. They are not typical of everybody. Most people, though a bit skeptical about the older generation, don't have the hatred of age or the authority problems that the great books deal with so enchantingly. But literature is a powerful force, and an excessive indulgence in it can give one the impression that the oldsters who are in power are out to get him. As a sophomore in my survey course said, after reading *Hamlet:* "This play helps me to see the adult world as a conspiracy." I have seen a great many Ph.D.'s with essentially the same attitude, though couched in subtler language. But sometimes, as they themselves grow older, they grow less vociferous about things geriatrical.

Our examination of the fabricated generation gap in literature should include the suggestion that the authority problems of artists are aggravated by something so simple as the way that old folks look. Everybody notices that when a person reaches his late twenties or early thirties, lines begin to form around his eyes. As he grows into middle age, these "crow's feet" multiply and become more elaborate, so that to a rather paranoid observer the eyes appear darker and more inaccessible, perhaps even evasive, devious, and threatening, though in fact the aging person's character hasn't changed much at all.

If we go to the other end of the spectrum and look at an infant's eyes, the absence of lines and the scanty or nonexistent eyebrows give us the impression of disarmed and wide-eyed wonderment, so that we don't feel threatened at all and may even feel superior. We can be sure that the child isn't hiding anything from us.

If we come to the middle of the spectrum and study the eyes of youth, we find a golden mean or compromise between the intricate eyes of age and the too-simple ones of infancy. In the rheumless look of youth we seem to perceive an openness and honesty. The eye of the young man or woman—or rather the flesh around that eye—is developed enough to be taken seriously, but it has neither the inane gaping wonderment of childhood nor the shifty evasiveness of age. It is, so we like to think, just right.

I believe that it is upon this profound triviality, the shape of an eye, that much of literature's hatred and distrust of age is based. It is interesting to notice how frequently creative writers describe in detail the eyes of their characters, as though this were the ultimate key to personality, the infallible guide to a person's schemes and desires. Eyes in the great books are described with such power and eloquence that as we read we can be lulled into forgetting how superficial and ignorant this method of judging character really is. Like the generation gap to which it is related, the meaningful or significant eye is for the most part a fabrication. It has some validity, but not much. Certainly not as much as the great books attribute to it.

Another strike against old people, as far as many authors are concerned, is that they don't move very smoothly. As they rise from chairs, walk, climb stairs, or sit down, their motions appear to be jerky, angular, and mechanical. Bowed and burdened with age, afflicted with rheumatism or arthritis, or at least with the stiffening of joints that begins in early middle age, the senior folk from forty onwards seem to move more like jerky apparatuses than like "human beings." In short, they look rigid and inflexible. It's seductively easy to make the transition from seeing them as physically inflexible to seeing them as mentally inflexible too. In the literature of the generation gap, the charge most often brought against the older generation—parents, guardians, rulers, officials, and sometimes anyone over forty or even thirty—is that they are unbending, uncompromising, stubbornly sticking to a single narrow track of thought or action. In tragic poems, plays, or novels, their supposed inflexibility has been blamed for such atrocities as the deaths of Pyramus and Thisbe, Romeo and Juliet, and any number of sweet youthful lovers down to the present day.

In comedy, the task of the hero is almost always to destroy the rigidity of the father-figures, if not to destroy the fathers themselves. More than one major critic (though Northrop Frye is the most eloquent on this topic) has argued that comedy concludes in a rightful victory for the flexible and tolerant attitudes of youth, after the senior authority figure has been derigidified or removed altogether. The customary inference is that tragedy, conversely, destroys the beautiful, flexible world of youth.

I'd like to offer two objections to this popular view of comedy as a revelation of the truth of youthful plasticity. First, no one has convincingly established that inflexibility is inherently bad. If the alleged rigidity of oldsters is merely a matter of non-malevolent consistency or habit of the type which develops as a natural outgrowth of living long enough to have been doing things the same way for a long time, then the charge of inflexibility so often hurled by authors against oldsters may be a meaningless one. But in too many of the great books the ultimate implication seems to be that the senior folk are bad merely because they don't bend. And too often it is really the kids, the Romeos and Juliets, who refuse to swerve. As an aside, it can be said that the poet's traditional—at least for the past two hundred years—hatred and fear of science and technology may be motivated by the same artistic hostility towards whatever seems unalterably or overly consistent, like the laws of physics or chemistry.

A second objection to the argument that comedy rightfully upholds the flexibility of youth, or that tragedy lamentably destroys it, is that it needs first to be proved that the younger generation is as fluid and elastic in its attitudes and behavior as literature cracks it up to be. We know that in actual life young people can be fantastically inflexible, as can be symbolized by the way so many of them dress alike, talk alike, think alike, listen to the same music, and worship the same heroes. This is essentially the way they've always been, and we are suspicious when the great books show them behaving some other way. The lithe and smoothly flexible movements of their sleek bodies need not fool us into equating physical with mental agility, any more than the stiff stumbling of oldsters need be equated with frozen stubbornness.

I don't know what the final truth is, but if I had to opt for one side or the other, I would say that I have seen more wisdom and flexibility in people over forty than in the Holden Caulfields and Portnoys down below. If the older generation has bungled the administration of the world, that is no guarantee that the youngsters could handle it any better. The great books are right in saying that the generations sometimes don't get along very well. The trouble is, our major authors too often go beyond this truism to mouth (in beautiful and convincing rhetoric) the fallacy that there are vast differences between the generations and that one is somehow much better than the other.

Part II

Seven
Avenues
to
Unawareness

Section 1

Misunderstanding Motivation

*The bizcacha has one very singular habit; namely, dragging
every hard object to the mouth of its burrow: around each
group of holes many bones of cattle, stones, thistle-stalks,
hard lumps of earth, dry dung, etc., are collected into an
irregular heap, which frequently amounts to as much as a
wheelbarrow would contain. . . . This habit of picking up
whatever may be lying on the ground anywhere near its
habitation, must cost much trouble. For what purpose it is
done, I am quite unable to form even the most remote
conjecture.*

—*Charles Darwin*, The Voyage of the Beagle

It is a truism about the academic world that the offspring of professors
are often problem children. The kids of the "humanities" faculties in
particular are some of the worst little hellions I've ever seen, and when
they reach adolescence they sometimes go off the deep end, like the
English professor's son who stole twelve cars one night and chained them
together in front of the Dean of Women's house and then went home and
put a bullet through his head, leaving a suicide note with only a terse
"fuck you" written on it. I don't know how the professor raised his son,
but I know that most people in the "humanities" feel that they are experts
on human behavior. Many of them like to raise their children according to
"theory," sometimes with disastrous Feverelean results. The basic
mistake they seem to make is assuming that human behavior makes more
sense than it actually does. Ancillary to this assumption is their belief
that if you merely show a person the path of "reason," he will follow it.

I know a well-dressed English professor, a specialist in American
Transcendental poetry, who frequently tries to "reason" with his seven-
year-old son. Recently he told me that he caught the boy riding a bicycle
that didn't belong to him. He gave his son a ten- or fifteen-minute lecture
on the importance and implications of property rights and ownership,
making his points clearly and logically, so that the boy would understand

42

and realize that it was for his own good and that of society that he respect the rights of others, particularly concerning property, mere possession of which was insufficient grounds for keeping or even using that property. Then he asked his son if the lesson were clear, and the boy nodded silently, as three or four of the neighborhood children listened and looked on.

As he told me the story, the professor seemed to think that he had handled the whole thing satisfactorily. He stressed the importance of explaining things to children rather than ruling over them by fiat and decree. Needless to say, he was appalled the next week when once again he caught his son on someone else's bike. He lectured the boy more sternly this time, delivering his speech with such vehemence that he drew a crowd of a dozen neighborhood kids. I asked him why he didn't go ahead and buy his son his own bicycle. He said that that would be giving in to society's materialism. He went on to say that he had cautioned his son many times about being too materialistic. Nor did he let him watch television, for TV was little more than a vast electronic conspiracy to get people to buy, buy, buy. All he wanted was to bring his son up to be a person who could achieve a serene spirituality by being able to shun the sirens of money and materialism. Then he quoted Thoreau: "A man is rich in proportion to the number of things which he can afford to let alone."

At this point I had had enough, so I made up an excuse to leave. As I walked across the campus, I thought about that professor's unfortunate son. What the hell did he care about lectures and theories? All he knew was that he had been humiliated in front of the neighborhood kids. I thought about all the other theorizing professor-parents I'd known and how stupid and dangerous they were; how they read too much about human nature and went around with the attitude that they could see farther and deeper than the average guy. The most dangerous kind of person, it seemed to me, was not the stupid man but the stupid man who is convinced that he's wise.

It's often said that art, literature in particular, gives us insight into human nature. Lately I have found it hard to go along with this proposition. I think literature gives us the illusion of insight rather than the real thing. It seems that every time we finish a great novel, poem, or play we come away with the feeling that we know, see, feel, and intuit signally more about man and the cosmos than we ever did before. But when we try to perceive or measure what we've gained, it seems to slip through our fingers like fine dry silt. Still we have the hard and fast impression that we've really gotten hold of something new and deep. The best writers always trick us this way; while telling us very little or nothing about ourselves, they succeed rhetorically in convincing us that they have taught us a great deal. I think they do this largely by "making sense" out of human nature, by imbuing it with a clever but fake logicality or "motivation," to use the term that all of us have often used in teaching "intro" or "survey" courses.

The great books are crammed full of "motivation." Up until the last few decades, the famous characters of the literature of the Western World have seldom done anything that didn't make perfect sense. To explain behavior every step of the way has been the function of our major authors from the time of Homer to almost the present day. I say "almost," because there is a new school of writing lately sprung up in America, England, and Europe which, refreshingly, allows man to be seen as much more irrational and arbitrary in his thoughts and actions. I am thinking in particular of such skillful irrationalists as Kurt Vonnegut, J. P. Donleavy, William Burroughs, and their German counterpart, Günther Grass. There are very few writers who anticipate this modern "irrationalist school." Some possibilities are Andre Gide (as in the gratuitous suicide of Boris in *The Counterfeiters*) and perhaps Stendhal, especially *The Red and the Black*. But by and large the view of man as genuinely irrational is a very recent development.

But we do most of our reading in earlier authors, which is to say that we spend most of our reading hours imbibing beautifully worked out, though questionable, analyses of human behavior. In effect the great books hammer and reinforce the thesis that man is thoroughly motivated and always has strong reasons for what he does. Even when characters go insane, like Shakespeare's Ophelia or Otway's Belvidera, their insanity is fully prepared for. The hearts of these two great ladies are so thoroughly broken that we would be surprised if they didn't go mad. And when they do, they tend to go right on speaking complete sentences. It would be difficult to find more sane treatments of insanity than in the great scenes of madness in front-rank English dramatists like Shakespeare, Otway, Kyd, Marlowe, Webster, and Ford.

However, the tradition of explaining, rationalizing, and making sense out of seemingly irrational acts goes back at least as far as the *Odyssey*. In Book IX of this renowned epic, the hero pulls what is surely one of the greatest blunders in literature. After blinding Polyphemus, the giant

Cyclops, Odysseus escapes from the Cyclops' island; and as he sails away, he shouts back, "Cyclops, if any man ever asks you how you got blinded, tell him it was done by Odysseus, the scourge of cities and Laertes' son, who lives on the island of Ithaca!" How could the hero be so foolish? Now that he has freely given his name, address, and ancestry to Polyphemus, it is a simple matter for the giant to relay this information to his father, Poseidon, the vindictive god of the sea. The price Odysseus must pay for so foolishly revealing his identity is to be condemned by the sea-god to wander for many years through strife and hardship.

Why did Odysseus do it? To Homer, the answer is simple. Odysseus did what any man might do after a fabulous victory in the face of impossible odds: he got so excited about winning that he momentarily lost control of himself. As Odysseus tells it, he couldn't restrain his "glorying spirit." So there! What at first seemed like an irrational act is blithely explained to make perfect sense! Once again we have seen that it is a main function of literature to rationalize man, to see to it that he is thoroughy motivated at all times, or to make sense out of his nonsense, if you will. The trouble with Homer's explanation of Odysseus' act is that like so many explanations in literature it denies the possibility that there may be no explanation at all. Man is a creature who so often acts in a wanton, unexpected way that any fair description of him must allow for his irrational side. To ignore it is to distort. The excessive "motivation" in so many of our great books functions to screen off one of the most important facets of human nature. We need to allow the possibility that Odysseus did what he did for no reason at all, or for the sheer unmitigated hell of it.

Once in a great while we come across a hero in earlier literature who does seem to be genuinely irrational, a hero for whom all explanations fail. Such a person is Shakespeare's Othello. There is no analysis or literary criticism in the world that can convincingly bridge the gap between his sweet gentle soul in the first half of the play and his homicidal howlings in the second half. I think a proper response to his complex character would be to let well enough alone and acquiesce in the possibility that he is simply doing what man has always tended to do: act in a way that makes no sense whatever.

What could be more human than to behave in a baffling, contradictory manner? Haven't we heard many times of murderers who were quiet and gentle until they surprised everyone by suddenly turning killer? No amount of investigation or analysis will ever completely explain the strange and grisly caprices of the Lizzie-Borden types, the Nathan Leopolds, and the Charlie Starkweathers. When all the final returns are in, all we can do is turn our palms upward, shrug, and say, "This is what people do." The trouble with the play *Othello* is not that it's irrational but that it's written in such a way that it causes critics to look for motivation for Othello. Every edition I've seen contains an introduction which grapples with this "problem" or "inconsistency" in the Moor's character. What we need instead is to furnish the student with no introduction, so that he may appreciate the stark fidelity with which Shakespeare portrays man, the craziest animal in the world.

It should be mentioned that the English language contains a number of works that merely feign or hint at man's irrational side, rather than showing us the real thing. A famous example is Edward Arlington Robinson's poem, *Richard Cory*. The hero is a rich man who appears to have everything conducive to happiness, but Robinson concludes by telling us that "Richard Cory, one calm summer night,/Went home and put a bullet through his head." Surely a central reason for this poem's fame is the shock effect of the suicide, which comes as a great surprise in the first reading.

However, if we reread it we can see that the poet has thoroughly prepared for Cory's death. The other characters in the poem, including the speaker, are the poor; they have no material wealth, but they do have hope and faith, as suggested in the passage that shows them waiting "for the light." It is this buoyance of soul that Richard Cory lacks. All the money in the world cannot compensate for his spiritual bankruptcy. Therefore we are finally not surprised at all by his suicide. There are hundreds of works of art like this, poems, novels and plays which merely hint at irrational behavior rather than face it head on. Some of the most powerful examples can be found among the medieval ballads—e.g., *Lord Randall* or *Sir Patrick Spens*. When we read this kind of literature, we seem always to be relieved when we finally discover "that the hero was satisfactorily motivated after all." It is this sense of relief that is our undoing, for it marks our acceptance of literature's dogma that man must always somehow make sense. Only rarely, and then perhaps only by accident, as in *Othello*, does a writer tell it like it is.

Until recently, the chief method used by writers to provide "motivation" for their characters was to establish in the first few pages a dichotomy between those time-honored rivals, passion and reason. It's interesting to note that many famous stories spring from an initial act of passion—the rape of Helen, the Fall of Adam and Eve, the lust of Lancelot for Guinevere, the murder of Hamlet's father, the adultery of *The Scarlet Letter.* Great narratives often begin with a physical display of excessive feeling, resulting in a displacement of man's rational faculties, which the next five hundred pages strive to rectify. The plot concludes when passion is spent and the order of reason is restored; when Odysseus is back on his throne at Ithaca; when Christ redeems man; when the Round Table is supplanted by the Holy Grail; when Denmark has been purged of rottenness; when Hester Prynne has paid for her transgression.

Works which show a less steady progress from passion to reason nevertheless derive much of their excitement from the apparent interplay of these two powerful ingredients in man. Frequent seesawing back and forth between judgement and emotion is characteristic of many heroes in the literature of the Western World, from the adulterous gods of Greek mythology to Myra Breckenridge. Even though the plot may begin not with an act of passion but with a decree of fate or with stern necessity—as in *Oedipus Rex* or *Les Misérables*—the conflict still tends to develop itself as a dialectic between passion and reason. In our hemisphere it can hardly be any other way, for Western man has always seen himself as split right down the middle: he is half soul, half body; half mind, half matter; half angel, half beast. It is no wonder that our great works of art are so frequently predicated on this supposed division. Most major authors of all centuries have relied on an image of man as divided, and they have concentrated their artistic energies on convincing their audiences of the validity of the image. And we have believed it.

We have believed it, but we shouldn't have. At least we shouldn't have gone along with the passion-reason dogma as readily and easily as we did, for it may be a dangerous distortion of man's makeup. I think that the best skepticism that can be brought against the Western dualistic view of humankind is to be found in the philosophy of George Santayana. In an essay called "The Comic Mask," he argues the possibility that reason is little more than another one of our "inherited passions." It seeks order, coherence, logicality, and consistency to the exclusion of everything else. Like any other passion, it can, if unchecked, seize and dominate the personality in a tyrannical way. When this happens on a mass scale, it can produce a society whose rage for order can have disastrous consequences, as in Nazi Germany.

Equipped with Santayana's insights, we need to look again at the kinds of orders established at the conclusions of a good many of our classics.

Returning to the examples used earlier, we would want to know if Odysseus is going to be a flexible and sensitive ruler—Odysseus who slaughters the suitors and hangs the unfaithful servants; Odysseus who in the administration of his court allows utterly no room for error on anyone's part. His methods remind me of a story about Hitler. One of his officers told him that burglaries were on the increase in Germany. "Next time a burgler is caught," Hitler said, "cut off his head." This was done and, the story goes, burglaries decreased. The point I am making in using these extreme examples is that the order or reason that is implemented or restored at the end of many great books is too often a small-minded, fanatical order, like the Pauline kind of Christianity, the rigid purity of the Holy Grail, Fortinbras' militaristic administration of Denmark, or the narrow sexual ethic adopted by Hester Prynne, who goes right on wearing the scarlet letter even though it's no longer required of her. In too many of our famous plots there is little real progress; what we have instead is the replacing of one tyrannical passion with another, which we foolishly label reason.

Much of our literature tries to appeal to us as artistic strife between man's rational faculties and his emotions, but sometimes it's more accurate to call it a free-for-all among a congress of weaknesses and shortcomings. I think it can be seen from what I've said that anybody who tries to learn very much about human nature from literature runs the risk of confusion compounded. The great books confuse readers by supplying excessive "motivation" for a creature who is more than sporadically irrational. Then the confusion is compounded by the bogus dichotomy between passion and reason.

Section 2

The Art of Categorizing Individuals and Oversimplifying Human Nature

And hence one Master-passion in the breast,
Like Aaron's serpent, swallows up the rest.
        —*Alexander Pope*, Essay on Man, *Epistle II*

Many English professors like to engage in bull sessions with their colleagues. In my experience, the favorite subject of these sessions was never literature, ideas, or academic affairs, but rather the various kinds of student behavior. The troublesome sorts of students were always the most fun to talk about. Occasionally we would get carried away to the point of writing fanciful essays or poems on the things the kids could do to get on our nerves. Some of these writings were published, and they usually appeared in *College English*, a periodical devoted to the pedagogical side of language and literature.

Some years ago this magazine printed a poem of mine, a sonnet about one of the more exasperating types, the student who misses a class and then shows up the next day and asks the professor what, if anything, went on last time. The student who asks about the class he missed could, I used to think, be divided into two categories: (1) the one who says, "What happened last time?" and (2) the one who says, "Did I miss anything?" The second one is by far the worst. The first one at least does the teacher the courtesy of assuming that something happened in class.

There were other types. There was the coed who hung around you after class, standing too close to you and trying to gather brownie points or maybe even seduce you, in order to get that "A" in the course. There was the "religious nut," who always intruded his Godly dogmas into the class discussion. There was the oversociable "inviter," a hard one to get rid of, who was always inviting his professors to his fraternity, his home, or to coffee, or the tavern. There was the "suggester," who was always coming up with suggestions about how you might improve your course, even though he was only a "C" student and scarcely seemed qualified to suggest anything. There was the dull "office rat," who hung around your office all the time, even though you were busy and he didn't have anything to say; every time you'd come back from a class, there he'd be, forlorn and lonely, waiting by your door. His opposite was the completely self-sufficient type, who would attend every class, sit in the rear, never take a note or say a word, leave immediately when class was over, and get straight "A's" on the exams. The self-sufficient type was probably no more exasperating than the type who sat in the front row and hogged too much of the class discussion, talking more for effect than for meaning or purpose. One of the most disappointing types, we all agreed, was the student who had a brilliant but hopelessly confused mind. This sort of person was capable of highly original insights but incapable of organizing them, thinking them out, or doing anything fruitful with them. Then there was the frowning bearded "questioner," crammed full of authority problems, who took nothing at face value, demanded that you back up absolutely everything you said, and was always delighted when he thought he'd caught you contradicting yourself.

There were literally dozens of student types that we could talk about. In addition to the ones described above, you could spend whole hours discussing other major types like the Neanderthal football player, the young right-winger who thought all professors were communists, the chronically forgetful and tardy student, the dumb sorority blonde, the subtle plagiarist, the crass business major, the paranoid minority-group student, the playboy, or the MAW (the well-meaning Middle-Aged Wife come back to school with her head full of clichés). From our professional point of view, there seemed to be no end to the procession of types: there we sat, shrewd observers of human nature, watching the endless parade and enjoying every minute of it. And when we tired of talking about student types, we could always turn our attention to society at large and discuss the many types to be found there—the blue-collar hard-hat, the Southern bigot, the downtrodden and threadbare public school teacher, the conniving politician, the angry Black, the aggressive and animalistic salesman, the liberal leftist, the black-jacketed motorcycle gang member, the Women's Lib gal, the smug aloof physician, and so on.

What we failed to realize in any of our bull sessions was that all of these types, inside and outside of the academic world, had something in common. What they had in common was the fact that they never existed, at least in the terms in which we conceived them. I'm sure now that if we'd ever taken the trouble to talk sympathetically and seriously with any "representatives" of these so-called types, which we never did, we would have learned that each of them was a singular and complicated individual who could not easily be placed in any general category of behavior. We would have learned how wrong we had been to sit there year after year and glibly reduce human beings to predictable automatons. We would have discovered, as Robert Coles points out in *The Middle Americans*, that it is practically impossible to categorize people, even the blue-collar ones whom we like to think of as delightfully simple and basic.

Sometimes when I think of this professional habit of stereotyping everybody under the sun, I think of it as a harmless pastime, an idle intellectual game with no real consequences. But at other times I see it as a dangerous game. Then it seems to me that this habit of so neatly categorizing our fellow human beings has had a hand in many of the great atrocities in the history of the world. It seems that nearly all pogroms and persecutions that we read about are based on false stereotypes, on sweeping simplistic assumptions about all kinds of groups—the Jews, the Philistines, the Christians, the Catholics, the Protestants, the Puritans, the Baptists, the Southern Baptists. With an equal felicity we also tend to typecast races, nationalities, and even neighborhoods. Like electricity, the mind of man tends to follow the course of least resistance, and it's a lot easier to generalize than to confront the bewildering variety of individual differences within even the most homogeneous group.

I think that the habit of stereotyping people is much more often a vice than a virtue, and I feel that the study of literature encourages this habit. Because of the way we are taught to teach literature in college, I wouldn't expect many people in the academic world to agree with me. Our customary approach is to try to present the great books as a kind of rapturous tribute to the uniqueness of the individual, with the hopes of making real individuals out of our students. But in fact as we teach or do research or publish articles, we inevitably begin to categorize the characters in famous novels, poems, or plays. This is what I was asked to do on my Master's and Ph.D. examinations. I remember a question on my M.A. exam which required me to discuss "the education of the hero in the eighteenth-century English novel." The phrasing of the question seemed to call for a finding of similarities, not differences, among the heroes, so I wrote a long essay in which I threw everyone from Moll Flanders and Evelina to Tom Jones and Humphry Clinker into the same essential category. When I was finished with my examination essay, I had closely defined a type—a kind of benevolent picaresque hero among whose chief functions is to serve as a vehicle for satirizing society. I passed the exam.

I wrote similar stereotyping essays for my Ph.D. general exams and dissertation. Then I went on to do the same thing in my scholarly articles and in my lectures. The fact that over the years I changed my critical approach several times didn't seem to make any difference. I always ended up typing the characters of literature. For a while I put everything in terms of Northrop Frye's four "pregeneric" personalities—alazon, eiron, buffoon, and agroikos. Before that I had tended to psychologize everything, lecturing for hours on the several types of schizoids that turn up in the great books, or smartly plunking characters into the generous categories of Freud. Before that I talked in terms of traditional literary types—the Misanthrope, the Avenger, the Malcontent, the Quixotic and Byronic heroes, the Guide of the Dream Allegory, the Wandering Jew, the Maimed Fisher King, the Tyrannical Father, the Picaro, the Melancholy Man, and so forth. I had also attempted at one time to categorize according to the theory of humors, which is the idea that the personalities of eccentric characters are dominated by having an excess of some natural trait. Thus a Miser, as in Molière's play of that title, was warped because he had an inordinate amount of the sense of economy that all of us are born with.

For one semester after another, I tried different approaches to literature, but they all had in common a strong tendency to see characters not as individuals but as types. It was rather inevitable that after several years of this kind of thinking I began to see real people that way too, a habit of mind that I still haven't broken completely. Upon meeting a new person, I still have to fight the urge to say to myself, "Ah, yes, he's the quiet, passive-aggressive type"; "Here's another one of these Southern Rednecks"; "There's a real endomorph for you"; or "O Lord, another right-wing, unimaginative engineer!" Even after knowing a person for a while, I have to fight the tendency to type him. I don't think I typed people so persistently before I was exposed to the great books, so I'm moved to the conclusion that there is something in the literature of the Western World that causes us to flatten human nature and individuality into an inaccurate, misleading, two-dimensional affair. It is not true that literature gives us insight into people; instead, in causing us to stereotype and categorize, it puts the blinders on.

I wish I were prepared to say what it is in the great books that encourages people to view each other in such a shallow way. I'm not sure what the answer is. Perhaps there is something in the basic nature of art which makes it impossible for a creative writer to place a human character within a fictional situation without dehumanizing him, so that in comparison with real humanity he becomes rather thin and flat, like the paper on which he is being described. Even when the character seems to be genuinely complicated, like Job, Hamlet, Raskolnakov, or Earwicker, somehow the effect of such a character on the reader is to uncomplicate the reader's view of life. It seems that the more elaborate the fictional character is, the more the audience feels the compunction to type and classify that character. Whether this phenomenon is caused by a basic contrariness in human nature or by some inherent defect in art, no one seems to know. The only thing that seems clear is that those who spend too much time around the great books spend too much time trying to categorize individuals. It's no use arguing with them. No matter what you say or how you say it, they've always seen you somewhere before.

Section 3

What's True of Me Is True of Everybody: How Literature Makes Us Project

Alice laughed. "There's no use trying," she said: "one can't believe impossible things."

"I dare say you haven't had much practice," said the Queen. "When I was your age, I always did it for half-an-hour a day. Why, sometimes I've believed as many as six impossible things before breakfast."

—*Lewis Carroll*, Through the Looking-Glass

"The mass of men lead lives of quiet desperation." How those words rang in my ears the first time I heard them! I was in my early twenties, just out of the Navy and back in college with an empty mind that eagerly awaited the input of new ideas. So that great sentence from Thoreau's *Walden* really impressed me. It had about it an aura of complete conviction and veracity. And the young professor who was teaching the course in the "American Renaissance" (Emerson, Thoreau, Melville, Hawthorne, Poe, etc.) fervently believed it too. After quoting it three or four times with a deep dramatic voice, he went on to elaborate on it: you take the average middle-class, middle-aged American, the "solid citizen" with the two cars, two kids, and two-level house with the two mortgages: if you could see deeply into his consciousness, chances are you would see a pretty unhappy individual. Under that placid, well-heeled exterior is a mass of frustration. Behind that polite, clean-shaven face there is a consciousness that once had excitement and imagination, high hopes and true

54

individualism. And look at it now: a dead brain and a dying spirit being carried around in a body that is still alive! What kind of life is that? Do you call that living?

At this point the professor would stop and glare around the room. We would feel embarrassed and lower our heads, as if to acknowledge that we too had been guilty of that cardinal sin, "quiet desperation," though to tell the truth we didn't know exactly what it was. That's how good the professor was. He was a spellbinder who could fire us with enthusiasm, so that up until two or three hours after class we felt eager to go out and spread the gospel of Thoreau—or whomever the professor had lectured about that day—throughout the world. After that, the enthusiasm would wear off and we would need to have our batteries recharged, which we would accomplish by going to class the next day.

Later on in my college career I became a bit disillusioned with that fireball professor, but one thing that did stay with me a good many years was my belief in the general validity of pronouncements on mankind by the major authors. (By "authors" I mean philosophers who wrote poetically as well as writers of fiction.) When Sophocles said, at the end of *Oedipus Rex*, "Call no man happy until, free from pain, he crosses into the world of the dead," it seemed to me that he told the absolute truth about the human condition. I thought Aristotle did too when he wrote that "learning is a great pleasure" (*Poetics*, Chapter 4), and the same with Boethius when he declared, in Book II of *The Consolation of Philosophy*, "The worst thing about misfortune is in *having been* happy," an idea enriched by Dante in Canto V of the *Inferno:* "There is no greater sorrow than to remember a time of happiness when one is in misery."

But most of my Great Pronouncements I got from the English masters. Chaucer had hit the nail right on the head when he capsulized my feelings about my career: "The lyf so short, the craft so long to lerne,/ Th' assay so hard, so sharp the conquering" *(Parlement of Foules)*. Needless to say, I gleaned dozens from Shakespeare: "Virtue is bold, and goodness never fearful" (*Measure for Measure*, III.i.214); "For sufferance is the badge of all our tribe" (*Merchant of Venice*, I.iii.111); "Silence is the perfectest herald of joy" (*Much Ado About Nothing*, II.i.219); "Nothing enboldens sin so much as mercy" (*Tempest*, III.v.3)—and so forth. Some of Milton's greatest ones were about women: "Wisest men/ Have erred, and by bad women been deceived;/ And shall again, pretend they ne'er so wise" (*Samson Agonistes*, 210). Pope was a storehouse second only to Shakespeare: "A little learning is a dangerous thing" (*Essay on Criticism*,

216); "Charms strike the sight, but merit wins the soul" (*Rape of the Lock*, Canto V, 34); and that great one in the Second Epistle of the *Essay on Man*, when he described *Homo sapiens* as "The glory, jest, and riddle of the world" (18). The English novelists were also warehouses of wisdom. Had not Fielding written that "it is not death, but dying, which is terrible" (*Amelia*, Book II, Chapter 4)? Had not Austen pointed out that "One half of the world cannot understand the pleasures of the other" (*Emma*, chapter 3)? Had not Trollope said, "We know that power does corrupt" (*The Prime Minister*, Chapter 68)? It seemed to me that such pronouncements were so thick in English literature, that the reader had to be careful where he stepped, in order to avoid tripping over an "ignorance is bliss" or slipping on a "better to have loved and lost," etc.

During the many years I spent being impressed with these Great Pronouncements, I spent very little time thinking about their philosophic viability. I did not, for instance, stop to consider that the trouble with "Charms strike the sight but merit wins the soul" is that many a soul has in fact been "won" with "charms." It may seem strange that somebody who was supposed to be intellectually sophisticated, as I was supposed to be, should for years live with all of this "wisdom" without ever putting any of it under critical analysis. But the reason is not far to seek: each of the Great Pronouncements is said so beautifully and eloquently that it tends to strike the reader with immediate conviction, catching him off guard and hitting him with such aesthetic force that he has little chance to think over what is actually being said. So powerful is the language of the major authors that we even forget the context of the pronouncement and nod in serious agreement with the "neither a borrower nor a lender be" speech in *Hamlet*, though it was spoken by that utter fool, Polonius. The point is, artistry and rhetoric can obscure or override just about any weakness of content.

But if we make the effort to look into the heart of a Great Pronouncement, we will see that the real trouble is usually that the author is *projecting*. This is a basic Freudian term which may be defined in layman's language: it means to externalize a thought so that it seems real, to make the mistake of thinking that what we see in ourselves is what is out there in everyone else. When he wrote *Walden*, Thoreau had on his mind the idea that he was leading a pointless and meaningless life, a life of "quiet desperation," to use his famous phrase. This egocentric feeling of frustration apparently raised his anxiety level high enough for him to resort to the gambit of projection. He quite naturally—and quite mistakenly—assumed that because he was leading a life of quiet desperation, everyone else was too.

I think the same can be said of many other famous writers. We have only to recall that writers are typically oversensitive and high strung. Such people are usually a little insecure, and their insecurity is quite likely to show up as a fear of being psychologically isolated: such a person finds it intolerable to be caught alone in a feeling or attitude, and therefore he is liable to invent a whole host of "believers" to share his sentiments with him. In the back of his mind he may know that no such host exists, and that relatively few share his view of things. But he can't face such a situation, so he is content to fool himself. In the process he fools us too. Because he is eloquent, gifted with the stupendous magic of words, it is no wonder that we are a poor match for him.

The better the author is, the more we need to say to him, "Speak for yourself." For that is precisely what the authors are doing, speaking for themselves, regardless of what character or mask or persona they're speaking through. When Shakespeare makes Hamlet, Lear, or Antony talk—or Richard the Third or Iago—he is saying things that in the heat of the creative moment are perfectly valid for himself, and while saying these things he is usually projecting too. It is interesting to notice that many of the most compelling pronouncements of "wisdom" in Shakespeare come from his great villains. We remember Iago's "Who steals my purse steals trash" or Richard the Third's "So wise so young, they say, do never live long." Probably both of these lines were true at one time for Shakespeare, and their eloquence tends to make them true for us. They go down so easily that we don't feel it necessary to examine them very closely.

In addition to examining Great Pronouncements more closely, we need to examine that which is pronounced on. Because great art usually appears to have strong universality to it, it readily seems to apply itself to all men. It seems quite natural to us that Thoreau, in attacking "quiet desperation," should accuse "the mass of men"—nearly everybody—of being guilty of it. I think back on the spellbinding professor who first told me about Thoreau's *Walden*, and I know now that he never took the trouble to get acquainted with that middle-aged, middle-class man whom he had lambasted semester after semester. In the years since my exposure to that professor, I have met a good many middle-class men, and men and women of all classes and backgrounds. I have known many of them well and only seldom did I find that seething frustration about which Thoreau wrote so beautifully and "convincingly."

It's my opinion that the professor had read too much of the kind of literature which insists that deep inside man there is something fighting to get out. Most of the great minds of the Western world seem to have gone along with this doctrine, all the way from Christ exorcising devils out of people and Zeus disburdening himself of Pallas Athena, down to Freud and his pronouncements on "repression" and "sublimation." Without such a doctrine, we would not have had many of the fine moments in our novels, poems and plays.

But our authors, and our psychiatrists too, are interested primarily in the unique individual, the singular and even the abnormal man or woman, not the average person. Because creative geniuses themselves tend to be "different," full of peculiarities and hangups, it's not surprising that they choose abnormal people like themselves to write about. The trouble lies not in their choice of subject matter but in their efforts to convince us that their subject matter is ourselves. Most of us, however, simply don't have those deep-seated drives and urges struggling to get out. We have our frustrations and secrets, of course, but they seldom reach the magnitude assigned to them by the major authors. This is another way of saying that although there is something universal in art, art is not as universal as we had thought.

Section 4

How Literature Separates Us from Our Feelings

Aschenbach folded his hands in his lap and looked out. He felt glad to be back, yet dissatisfied with his changing moods and his ignorance of his own actual desires.
—Thomas Mann, Death In Venice

Most of us are old enough to remember how we felt on November 22, 1963, that black day when President John F. Kennedy was assassinated. Regardless of our politics, we felt a great hollowness in our stomachs, put there by the emotions of sorrow and outrage. We weren't good for much the rest of the day, and the president of the little college where I was then teaching had the heart to cancel classes until the next morning.

I remember the faces of students, red and filled with tears. One boy about nineteen years old, who had played the cynic in my freshman English class, came to me and said, "This is a terrible thing." That unsophisticated but heartfelt sentence showed that he knew when to put his satirical intellect aside and turn to his emotions. He had ready access to his feelings, he used them, and he wasn't ashamed of it. In this respect he was very unlike some "humanities" teachers at a nearby university.

The president of this larger and more sophisticated institution did not cancel classes on the day of the assassination. Instead he left things to the discretion of the individual faculty members. Most of the professors called off their classes, except for a small group of junior faculty teaching the "humanities." Several of these were English professors, new on the job and eager to do well. I heard that one of them told his survey-of-English-literature class that a mere assassination was insufficient reason

59

for calling off the pursuit of truth. He didn't argue from the point of view that keeping busy helps us through times of sorrow and rage. Rather he argued that the class must go ahead in the name of the arts. The students were appalled, but he kept them there for the full fifty minutes while he lectured to them on some passages in Shakespeare.

I wasn't told what parts of Shakespeare the professor talked about that day. Maybe he was dealing with *Hamlet*, perhaps with some of the fine soliloquies in that play, like the one beginning "Oh that this too too sullied flesh would melt" or the greatest of all, "To be or not to be." In any case, if he had been doing a good job, and he probably was, he would have been calling his students' attention to the poet's ability to make beautiful and sensitive reference to a broad scale of human feelings.

Shakespeare's genius in playing upon the complex keyboard of emotion can be illustrated by the "To be or not to be" soliloquy. In this celebrated thirty-five line speech, the poet refers to over thirty distinct areas of human response that can legitimately be called emotions:

> To be, or not to be—that is the question:
> Whether 'tis nobler in the mind to suffer
> The slings and arrows of outrageous fortune
> Or to take arms against a sea of troubles
> And by opposing end them. To die, to sleep—
> No more—and by a sleep to say we end
> The heartache, and the thousand natural shocks
> That flesh is heir to. 'Tis a consummation
> Devoutly to be wished. To die, to sleep—
> To sleep—perchance to dream: aye, there's the rub,
> For in that sleep of death what dreams may come
> When we have shuffled off this mortal coil,
> Must give us pause. There's the respect
> That makes calamity of so long life.
> For who would bear the whips and scorns of time,
> Th' oppressor's wrong, the proud man's contumely,
> The pangs of despised love, the law's delay,
> The insolence of office, and the spurns
> That patient merit of th' unworthy takes,
> When he himself might his quietus make
> With a bare bodkin? Who would fardels bear,
> To grunt and sweat under a weary life,
> But that the dread of something after death,
> The undiscovered country, from whose bourn
> No traveller returns, puzzles the will,
> And makes us rather bear those ills we have
> Than fly to others that we know not of?

Thus conscience does make cowards of us all,
And thus the native hue of resolution
Is sicklied o'er with the pale cast of thought,
And enterprises of great pitch and moment
With this regard their currents turn awry
And lose the name of action.—Soft you now,
The fair Ophelia!—Nymph, in thy orisons
By all my sins remembered.

There is a feeling of uncertainty in the opening line, "To be or not to be, that is the question." There is outrage in "the slings and arrows of outrageous fortune." There is resignation in "to die; to sleep;/ No more." There is sorrow in the reference to "heartache." The "thousand natural shocks" conveys the emotion of being shocked. "'Tis a consummation devoutly to be wished" suggests a feeling of resolution or certainty. There is the feeling of surprise that comes with sudden discovery in "aye, there's the rub!" The emotion of fear is there when Hamlet thinks of those "dreams" that might occur after death. "Shuffled off this mortal coil" arouses the emotions associated with strife and struggle. A feeling of reverence is conveyed by "there's the respect." Both aggression and scorn are evoked by "the whips and scorns of time." There is a sense of injustice in "the oppressor's wrong," and the arch-emotion of pride shows up in "the proud man's contumely." "The pangs of despised love" easily suggests disappointment and anguish, while the emotion of frustration is carried in "the law's delay." A feeling of brazeness comes before us in "the insolence of office," to contrast with the calmness of "patient merit" in the next line. Deep despair combines with horror in the idea of making a suicidal quietus "with a bare bodkin." What could be more attuned to the emotion of weariness than the line "to grunt and sweat under a weary life"? There is a feeling of panic in the reference to fleeing from this world's evils "to others that we know not of." Disgust with the self emerges in the familiar "thus conscience does make cowards of us all." Revulsion, melancholy and lethargy are beautifully combined in "sicklied o'er with the pale cast of thought," which contrasts with the feelings of anticipation and eagerness in the "enterprises of great pitch and moment." Just then Ophelia appears, plunging Hamlet into feelings of guardedness and vigilance: "soft you now!" But he quickly shifts to feelings of admiration and love in his reference to her as "the fair Ophelia!" The great speech concludes with suggestions of the emotions of faith and hope: "nymph, in thy orisons/ Be all my sins remembered." It seems somehow redundant when in the next line Ophelia asks Hamlet how he feels.

The professor might have told his classes, and he would have been right, that no writer ever described man's emotions more richly and delicately than Shakespeare. And as they sat there and tried to listen to their teacher, the sad, shocked students must have sensed a contradiction between the delicacy of feeling in Shakespeare and the insensivity of the oaf who went right ahead and held his classes on that dark day.

Perhaps he was born an oaf. But it's also possible that the arts turned him into one. If it's true that many of the greatest literary works scrutinize emotions, it's also possible that they scrutinize them to death. Without denying that it's important to think about our feelings, we should consider the possibility that an excessive concentration on feelings may have the paradoxical effect of denying access to those feelings.

A person can think so long and hard about feelings that finally he actually doesn't know what he feels or hardly feels at all. Too much medicine will kill us. We in the "humanities" are amazed when we learn that our colleagues can be nasty, boorish, and inhumane. Vigorously we point to the contradiction between this kind of behavior and the supposed virtues of the arts. We need instead to consider the arts as the possible cause of callousness in people.

Section 5

How Reading Makes Us Lazy

Then came Sloth all beslobbered, with two slimy eyes,
"I must sit," said he, "or else I will nap.
I cannot stand or stoop or kneel without a stool.
If I were lying in bed, unless my rear-end forced me,
No ringing would make me rise till I was ready to dine."
— The Vision of Piers Plowman *(B), Passus V*

A few years ago, if someone had said to me that art makes people lazy, I would have thought he was badly mistaken. Today I'm not so sure. I tend to be an indolent person, though the books I read have a way of making me forget this fact. Lately I have begun to suspect that in addition to making me ignore my own laziness, literature actually makes me lazy. What initially made me suspicious wasn't anything I had read recently but rather my memories of reading I did long ago. Like many others, in recent years I have succumbed to the nostalgia that is a current fad in the pop culture of our nation. I have been dwelling on my youth, a chaotic and irresponsible period in which I actually read what I *wanted* to read.

When I was in junior high school, one of my favorite writers was Will James (not to be confused with the philosopher William James!). He was the author of numerous horse-and-cowboy novels like *Smoky, Lone Cowboy,* and *Big Enough.* James was a comic writer, not in the sense of laughter but in the sense of rewarding his heroes at the end with money, horses, ranches, or girls, after those heroes had struggled through two hundred pages of unruly nags, cattle stampedes, broken legs, and bad weather.

As I think back on the hours I spent reading Will James, it is mostly a vague memory now, but there is one thing I recall clearly, and that is the

63

feeling of having worked. James was a kinesthetic writer. He could make you imaginatively dig your heels into the ground as you tried to subdue your half-tame pony long enough to get a saddle on him. He could make you feel a jolting saddle under your crotch. He could make you strain every muscle to get out from under a bronco that had fallen on you. To finish a Will James novel was to have done a full day's work. You felt thoroughly wrung out and ready for a rest. James was so skillful that he could make you forget that you had not worked at all. He could at least temporarily remove from your mind the fact that all you had done was sit on your posterior and read a novel. He was a master at giving his readers the illusion that they had done something.

I think that what happened to me as I read Will James continued to happen to me in my later reading, though in a more subtle way. When I began to read writers who were less obvious, less physical, and not at all kinesthetic, I still had that sensation of having acted or worked or done something. But this sensation was fainter now, and moreover it tended to be pushed out of the spotlight of my consciousness by the more pressing business of literary criticism demanded of me in graduate school and in my "profession."

Perhaps it's time to lay criticism aside in order to look again at this elementary sensation of having done something. First of all, I notice that I get it not only from the novel or drama of action but also from the quieter sorts of literature. A lyrical poem like Marvel's *To His Coy Mistress*, although it can't give us the Will James saddle-jolt, certainly gives us the impression of having argued our heads off in order to get a beautiful woman to go to bed with us.

From Marvel it is only one more step to the kind of literature that gives us the impression, not of having done something, but of having thought or felt something. Maybe one reason why Gray's *Elegy Written in a Country Churchyard* is said to be the most famous poem in the language is that it succeeds so beautifully in giving us the illusion that we have emoted over the graves of obscure villagers—when in fact we have done no such thing. It's possible that when we finish the *Elegy* we are so steeped in "having felt" that we can feel no more. Literature thus may sometimes have the weird effect of turning us away from the very thing with which it wants us to sympathize. It is Gray's objective, or one of his objectives, to get his readers to commiserate with the lower classes; and in successfully giving us the illusion of having done so, he ensures that we don't. Armed with the feeling that we have already performed, we can't see the need for performing any further. Lincoln said that Harriet Beecher Stowe was the little lady who started the Civil War. But insofar as she succeeded in making us feel sorry for Uncle Tom and outraged by his plight, she might be said to have delayed the war. An underlying message of much literature is that a substitute for action, a sensation of having acted, is better than action itself.

I used to be amazed at the inertia of many people in the "humanities." For every hard-working go-getter, there seemed to be a dozen goof-offs: profs who hadn't read a book in years; teachers who wouldn't prepare for class or correct their papers; students who because they couldn't get their work done piled up scandalous numbers of "incompletes"; people who loafed and lingered for eons in graduate school and still didn't get their Ph.D.'s. I think it was art that helped to make them that way. Even if they were naturally inclined to be lazy, literature encouraged and added to their laziness on all levels—physical, intellectual, and emotional. And while it was making them lazier, it was convincing them that they were up and doing.

Section 6

Our High Toleration of Incompetence

Here lies one who meant well, tried a little, failed much:—
surely that may be his epitaph, of which he need not be
ashamed.

—Robert Louis Stevenson, Across the Plains
(XII "A Christmas Sermon," iv)

Any English professor who teaches an introductory course in famous
epics or tragedies takes upon him the burden of explaining a number of
"foreign" terms to his students. Chief among these might be such old
standbys as *hamartia, in media res, catharsis, epic simile, catastrophe,*
muse, and *hubris.*

I used to enjoy explaining the last one, *hubris,* more than any of the
others, because it was the one that the class got the most excited about.
When I told them that it meant "overweening pride," they would start
arguing about whether it was a virtue or a vice. One group would say that
pride was the motivating factor that was responsible for man's great
achievements, such as the locomotive, the automobile, the airplane, and
the manned space rocket. Those in the other camp would counter by
saying that this prideful urge to do the spectacular was man's undoing and
downfall—look at gunpowder and the atom bomb, not to mention
pollution from the "achievements" named by the first group.

At the time I thought it was a healthy thing, this open discussion of
hubris and its implications for modern man. I still believe that, but I'm
sorry we didn't discuss another implication of overweening pride. The
truth is, it didn't even occur to me at the time, because those were the
Halcyon days before I got disillusioned about the arts. It occurs to me

66

now that the significant thing about pride or *hubris* in literature is not its "achievements" or tragic falls but its incompetence: what a great many striving heroes of literature have in common is simply that they are bunglers. They can't seem to carry out the jobs assigned to them without goofing up in some disastrous way.

It's hard to believe that people can study literature year in and year out without imbibing at least a little of the idea that incompetence is acceptable, if not actually attractive, as a way of life.

The most renowned stories of the Western World are frequently built around a central bungler whose incompetence has the effect of injuring a good many around him. An obvious example is the myth of Adam and Eve. Their task was simple, merely to loaf and to keep away from the Tree of Knowledge of Good and Evil. But they blew it. It's interesting to notice how many legends or myths begin with the mistakes or bad judgments of some primordial butterfingers like Pandora or the builders of Babel. Many plots could not exist without the stumbles and foul-ups of the main character. Where would much of the excitement of the Trojan War have come from, if it had not been for Achilles' stupid refusal to accept Agamemnon's peace offer in Book IX of the *Iliad*? Wouldn't Beowulf have been a duller story if the mead-soaked hero had kept his eyes open instead of slumbering through the murderous visit of Grendel's mother? What if Roland had blown his horn, which he so pig-headedly refused to do? Who can imagine King Lear as a wise father and administrator, Hamlet as a competent criminal investigator, Antony as a practical military commander, or Macbeth as a shrewd politician? Where would Milton have gotten his passionate material for *Paradise Lost* if Satan had not misplanned and misjudged his assault on the Almighty?

It seems to be one of the many built-in restrictions of literature that it often must base itself on incompetence. And many a time the writer's artistry has the effect of making incompetence attractive. This is especially true of comic characters. We all love Falstaff, Don Quixote, Joseph Andrews, Huckleberry Finn, and even Babbitt, though most of the time they can't seem to do anything right. We seem to admire the more serious ones, the Beowulfs and the Hamlets, in spite of their propensity to drop the ball.

Though the theme of incompetence is most noticeable in narrative literature, it also plays a part in lyric poetry. In this kind of writing the hero is often the speaker or the poet himself. One of the roles most frequently played is that of the unsuccessful lover. The voice speaking in a love poem usually belongs to a person who has (1) completely failed to win his lady, (2) has not yet succeeded in winning her, or (3) has won her but does not feel secure or victorious in his love. Though these three types of unsuccess can be found in poetry of many centuries and places, the English Renaissance offers some of the finest examples.

Thomas Wyatt's *They Flee From Me* is a beautiful admission of defeat in which the speaker reveals his vindictive temper, which probably causes him to mishandle the affair: "But since that I so kindly am served,/ I fain would know what she hath deserved." Shakespeare is another writer who casts himself in the role of a lover who can't seem to succeed in love. In sonnet after sonnet he pleads for a loving response but seldom seems to get it. Finally, in some of the later sonnets (though the chronology is uncertain), he becomes cynical and sings of the ugly Dark Lady. "Sour grapes" and "poor loser" are clichés that apply here, as the Shakespearean lover tries to blame the world and human nature for his own ineptitude in the art of wooing.

Some of the most famous Renaissance love poems are those in which the speaker has *not yet succeeded: Come Live With Me and Be My Love, Drink to Me Only With Thine Eyes, Gather Ye Rosebuds While Ye May, To His Coy Mistress.*

A lover who has won but feels insecure in his victory shows up frequently in Donne's *Songs and Sonnets.* Even when he *says* he feels secure, the *way* he says it makes us doubt him, as in the *Valediction Forbidding Mourning.* This ingenious poem is so full of farfetched metaphors, tension, paradox, and general *strain* that we come away from it completely unconvinced that Donne's love is as inviolable as he says it is.

Looking at the several stances taken by speakers in love poems, we are led to the conclusion that we are once again in the presence of that bad penny, incompetence. It's hard to reach any other conclusion when so many poetic voices begin by identifying themselves as thorough-going lovers and then promptly proceed to fail in love. To the objection that such a reading takes the poems in the wrong spirit, we may say that we are merely looking at the facts. There may be a success of poetic artistry, but what actually happens in the poem is unsuccess brought on by the inability of the hero to perform that which he is purportedly able to do.

This is the situation in much literature, whether poetry or prose, for without a bungle or a mistake it is not easy to have conflict, movement, or plot. To have these is to have a situation in which the chips are down; and when they're down, even the slightest incompetence will be blatant and glaring. We know that incompetence is everywhere in real life; it's just that it usually doesn't show unless some emergency occurs. We can't test our firemen without a fire, our policemen without a crime. But perpetual emergency is the state of affairs in virtually any piece of literature. Therefore there is always some opportunity for the hero to reveal his incompetence.

In recent novels there is more opportunity than ever, for no age ever valued incompetence the way ours does. The number of modern antiheroes who are unable to do their jobs is impressive. Some of the more artistic failures are Harry Levin of *A New Life*, Yossarian of *Catch-22*, Rabbit of *Rabbit Run*, and Sebastian Dangerfield of *The Ginger Man*. In each of these books the message appears to be that the job isn't worth doing anyway. But somehow that seems to beg the question of whether incompetence is a virtue. A further smokescreen is thrown up by the author's habit of implying that although the hero is all thumbs, he has some saving grace, such as that shopworn favorite, "refusal to go along with the establishment" or its companion, "integrity of character."

It may sound absurd to say that people can be infatuated with incompetence, but I have seen just such persons in the "humanities." I remember one middle-aged professor at a major university, a man very much respected in his field of Renaissance English. I had several classes from him, and there was never any doubt in my mind about his brilliance in his particular field. He was a charming teacher, and he used to entertain us by revelling in his incompetence in all fields outside of his own. "Oh," he would declare, "I'm a *complete* ignoramus about American literature; I simply can't *grasp* Middle English; the Victorians completely *escape* me"—and so forth.

More than that, he enjoyed his incompetence in fields outside of English. He was so poor in math, and so proud of it, that he would make quite a show out of not being able to figure out what date the midterm exam would be on, if it were more than a few days from today's date. He wasn't putting us on; he really was incompetent outside of his field and pleased as punch about it. I think his reasoning was that because he was a whiz in one area he could be weak in all others. There is an analogy between this "one saving grace" approach to things and the attitude, widespread in comic literature, that being a good example of the vagaries of "human nature" excuses one from being a good example of anything else. Such is the raison d'être of the Wife of Bath, Lazarillo de Tormes, Falstaff, Tom Jones, Candide, and Tom Sawyer.

By the way, the professor referred to above excused us, his students, for being rather incompetent in the field he taught. He had a reputation as an easy grader. Since my student days, I have seen a great many like him—teachers and students in the arts who have an enormous tolerance for incompetence in a great many areas. I see that I have had this tolerance in myself, when late at night, toward the end of a huge stack of student papers, I have scribbled "A" where it should have been "B," "B" where it should have been "C."

Intentional in the comic, unintentional in the serious, incompetence is everywhere in literature. There really is something rather brain-softening about art. If it makes us tolerant, it makes us tolerant of the wrong things. Incompetence is one of these.

Section 7

The Virgin
and the Crowbar:
Increasing
Our Hostility

Such dim-conceived glories of the brain
Bring round the heart an indescribable feud;
So do these wonders a most dizzy pain,
That mingles Grecian grandeur with the rude
Wasting of old Time—with a billowy main,
A sun, a shadow of a magnitude.
—John Keats, On Seeing the Elgin
Marbles for the First Time

For a long time the shabby young man stands there, staring at the statue.
He is unnoticed by the guards and the many tourists coming and going in
the huge cathedral. The statue is a life-size Virgin Mary, seated, with her
dead son gracefully sprawled across her lap. She gazes down at the
crucified young god with an expression of such delicacy and beauty that
it's hard to look at her face very long without turning away. But the young
man stares. His posture is crouched and tense, like that of a person about
to do something violent. Suddenly he acts. From inside of his dirty
overcoat he draws a crowbar and starts smashing the statue. The chips fly
as he swings again and again, shouting "I am the Savior!" The tourists
and guards gape in disbelief at the madman. Then the guards rush in to
subdue him and take him away. It's too late. Having miraculously come
unharmed through four centuries of mankind's destructiveness, the statue
is now severely damaged—even beyond repair, according to some
experts.

For some reason most of the damage is around the Virgin's upper body
and face, though she still has traces of her gaze of indescribable beauty.

71

The man with the crowbar called himself Christ, as if the figure in her lap had usurped his place. But it seems strange that he concentrated his attack on the Mary rather than on the Jesus, which was completely unharmed. Perhaps his vandalistic act was a gesture against the Roman Catholic church, which is often symbolized by the Virgin Mary. Or perhaps, if we adopt a Freudian interpretation, his act had nothing to do with religion at all, being a manifestation of his subconscious hatred of his own mother. Because he seems to be suffering from some sort of mental illness, it's difficult to say exactly what caused him to attack that priceless statue. Any theory about his behavior is potentially as valid as any other.

One possibility is that the madman was angered neither by religious matters nor by his mother, but by art. It's interesting to note that for his attack he chose one of the five or six best pieces of sculpture in existence. If his problem had been strictly religious or "Oedipal," he could have used any number of artistic or nonartistic objects as targets for his fury. But he chose the lovely statue. It is enough to make one suspect that there is something in the basic nature of the plastic arts that encourages people to be angry or hostile, even though they may channel or sublimate these feelings in quiet ways which are acceptable to society. Part of the trouble with the madman was not that he was angry but rather that he couldn't find an acceptable outlet for his anger.

Another part of his trouble was that he lived too late in history. There have been certain times and cultures in which statue smashing or literal iconoclasm was acceptable or even requisite. We think of the zealous Reformationists in the abbeys or the barbarians invading ancient Greece and Rome, clobbering every piece of sculpture in their path. Incidentally, those old barbarians usually went for the face: a good many statues coming down to us from classical times have relatively intact bodies but faces smashed beyond all recognition, and many of these ancient pieces are headless, a tradition that was revived a few years ago when someone decapitated the famous little Hans Christian Andersen mermaid that sits in the harbor at Copenhagen. We were all appalled, partly because we didn't realize that whoever did it was merely responding to an age-old anger that any well-executed statue is capable of provoking. It was as natural an anger as that felt by Moses when he flung his crude stone tablets down at the meticulously finished golden calf. Because first-rate sculptures are potentially infuriating, we usually have to keep them locked up and out of reach. If we leave them unattended in public places, it isn't only the pigeons we have to worry about.

So far we have been talking about situations in which the anger provoked by the statue is turned back on the statue itself. Another common situation is for the anger to be directed toward something or someone nearby or associated with the statue. Travelers and anthropologists have told us about so-called "primitive rituals" in which bloody acts like animal or even human sacrifices are committed at the feet of some gigantic piece of sculpture with a look on its high-up face of impassive inpenetrability. In some rituals the statue itself is destroyed after the sacrificers are through with it. Through the years there has always been a close association between crime or aggression and sculpture, as can be seen in the pilfered Egyptian tomb, the war monument, or petty larceny like André Malraux's stealing the Khmer statues in Indochina some years ago. The signs in the British Museum tell us everything about the statues there, except how they were stolen from other countries. (However, there is one sign on the Elgin Marbles which strains to "justify" or "explain" how the Earl of Elgin had to get those marbles out of Greece before they were completely destroyed.) So close is the association between sculpture and aggression that people often "torture" statues to symbolize their hatred, as in the use of dolls to put the "hex" on someone or in the campus ritual of hanging the football coach in effigy after losing a big game. However, when we want to commend or congratulate someone, we don't use dolls or effigies. We go directly to the real person himself and hoist him on our shoulders or put him in a parade. We don't usually build a statue of him until after he's dead.

What is it that gives a piece of sculpture the power to move us toward anger or hostility? I'm not sure what the answer is. For a while I thought it had a great deal to do with the fact that the best or the most famous statues usually have some association with violence or bloodshed, like the following: The Laocoön. The Sphinx (devourer of men). The Winged Victory. The Discus Thrower (this was once a weapon). The Dying Gaul. Any number of beautifully carved crucifixes. Michelangelo's Pietà (the aftermath of violence), his Moses and his David (both foreshadowings of violence). Cellini's Perseus with the Head of the Medusa. Rodin's Gates of Hell. Many of the attenuated and tortured shapes of Giacometti. My theory was simply that any good plastic suggestion of violence could evoke corresponding emotions in those who looked at it. One trouble with my theory, however, was that it seemed that people could also become angry by looking at nonviolent sculpture, like the Colossus of Memnon, the Venus of Milo, or Rodin's The Thinker. So while not completely eschewing my old answer, I had to play it down somewhat and look around for some new answers.

What I finally came up with was the possibility that statuary makes us angry because it partakes of life but doesn't have to pay any of the penalties. The Virgin Mary with her dead son in her lap is incredibly lifelike, almost breathing and moving; but it is serenely exempt from all the natural shocks that flesh is heir to. It knows no real sorrow, pain, or death; it was here four hundred years ago and will be here four hundred hence. Yet it seems animated and seems to breathe the air we breathe. In the backs of our minds we sense a blatant double standard. It doesn't have to suffer or die but we do. We are "justly" angry at such a situation, even though our anger may be purely subconscious and may emerge only in the form of socially acceptable acts. The madman with the crowbar was more direct in his approach. He tried to do away with the double standard by making the statue pay the penalties of life; in his madness he tried to make it know suffering and death as he himself would know them.

I've rattled on about sculpture longer than I should have. I wanted to discuss it because I think that what happens with sculpture is essentially the same with the other arts, only it's much easier to see it in the physical, three-dimensional presence of sculpture. It's almost as easy to see it in painting, and less easy than that to see it in literature. It's more difficult to see it in music. Nevertheless, all of these artistic media when exploited by genius can give us the impression that they live today and yet are timeless and exempt from the bad parts of life.

Literature in particular tries to be above all a representation of life, full of "deeds and language such as men do use." But while we marvel at the author's skill in giving his work a sense of life we also realize that the book we hold in our hands is an inanimate thing which might have been held by someone who died before we were born, or that the story in the book may have been chanted around a fire three thousand years ago by men who even then were old and near death. The excitement that can rise up in us as we read the great books may be partly due to the ambivalence between these two artistic ingredients of life and lifelessness. If the conflict is strong enough, as it is in the classics of the Western World, it may kindle in the backs of our hearts that old wrath, that sense of outrage and indignation at something that can be alive, as we are alive, and yet be eternal.

If we are reasonably well-adjusted human beings, we don't throw the book at the wall or take a crowbar to it. Indeed, we probably don't even know we're angry, because our anger is so smoothly being channeled into socially acceptable acts. But the anger is still there, and what is socially acceptable can at the same time be very destructive. I think this is true of most of the criticism or scholarship we write about literature. It is of course socially acceptable, even mandatory, in our "profession" of the "humanities." However, it too often damages the novel, poem, or play that it's supposed to illuminate. The kind of criticism and scholarship that regularly appears in the learned journals functions as a crowbar in two ways. (1) By shedding light on literature, which is its avowed purpose, it may in fact illuminate the work, but in doing so it too often pollutes the atmosphere of magic and mystery on which so much of the power of the great book depends. It's hard to believe that either the world or the work of art would be better off if some scholar were to tell us precisely what's on Hamlet's conscious and subconscious minds. But that's exactly what scholarship and criticism have been working at for centuries. (2) By their habit of causing a mass of learning to accrete around a masterpiece, scholars and critics have driven a wedge between the audience and the work, and this scaring-off tactic can only harm the work. Although criticism does a good service in calling our attention to a piece of literature, the process never seems to stop there. Instead, the accretion of knowledge and illumination continues, until we either know too much about it and so are tired of it, or can't penetrate the moraine of scholarship and so are tired of it.

The old barbarians, when they stormed into Greece and Rome and smashed the statues, usually went for the head. If they couldn't knock it off they could still obliterate the face with a few good strokes of the battle-axe. There is an analogy between the barbarism of the "Dark Ages" and the barbarism of modern literary criticism or scholarship: they both go for the face or the head. The "head" of a novel, poem or play is its most powerful and intricate passage or passages. In the play *Hamlet*, the "head" is the renowned "To be or not to be" soliloquy, and it is at this head that most scholars and critics have aimed their crowbars. I'm afraid that I was right in there with them when I wrote about that soliloquy in the part of this book that deals with the way literature severs us from our feelings. What made me choose it to write about was not only my thesis but also my belief that the "To be or not to be" speech had more life and eternity in it than anything else in the play. I'm sure I managed to deaden it somewhat with my analysis of it. For the truth is that in spite of all of their careful phraseology and fine microscopic distinctions, literary criticism and scholarship in their ultimate effects on the work of art are blunt and crude instruments, as rough and random as the madman's crowbar.

We noticed earlier that the anger provoked by statues is sometimes directed not at the statues themselves but at something or someone nearby. The same is true of literature, which may help to explain certain types of overreactions commonly observed among English professors. When I was in school I witnessed a number of situations in which professors got angry at students for misconstruing passages in the great books. At the time, I was baffled by the disparity between the triviality of the student's transgression and the magnitude of the teacher's anger. Now, years later, I'm pretty sure that the teachers, even unbeknownst to themselves, had already been provoked by the piece of literature before the class started. They were primed and ready to pounce on the first student who was hapless enough to misread or misunderstand something in the great books, like the young man who in all sincerity gave a sexual interpretation of the first line of Spenser's *Faerie Queene:* "A gentle knight was pricking on the plain."

Yes, art can make us angry, and hostile too. Apparently it has had this function from the very beginning, when it arose as song, dance and picture for the purpose of whipping up an enthusiastic hostility in the hunters, on whom the survival of the tribe depended. The purpose of those early painters, musicians, and poets was not to soothe the savage breast but to supercharge it with wrath and ferocity.

Part III

Five
Avenues
to
Unhappiness

Section 1

Does Literature Cause Insanity?

I have never in all my life seen so many weirdos.
—Remark made by a graduate student
attending his first Modern Language
Association conference

There was a tall poet at a major university who periodically would go insane. He was an "academic" poet, nearly famous, and employed as a professor because he brought prestige to the university and because he couldn't make enough money from his verse to support himself. I don't know how directly the campus atmosphere contributed to his crackups and breakdowns, but he regularly chose the classroom as the location in which to start one.

Once, on a fine fall morning, when school had been in session about two weeks, he walked into his 9:00 A.M. Elizabethan poetry class and blew up. He began the class by reading aloud from Sir John Davies' *Orchestra*, but after a few minutes (at the part beginning "Behold the world, how it is whirled around"), his voice went hoarse, and his hands began to shake. Then, as the stunned students looked on, he threw down the book and began cursing and swearing at Sir John Davies (who died in 1626). "Who are *you*," he shouted, "who are *you* to talk about order and harmony? What do *your* deaf ears know about the music of spheres? Fuck *you*, Sir John Davies!" By this time several boy students had jumped up and run out of the room. (All the girls stayed; for some reason they're tougher in this sort of thing.)

Apparently word soon got to the English Department office, because within a few minutes the department chairman, himself a big man, and

78

another burly professor appeared at the door. Together they subdued the flailing arms and loud voice of the mad poet. They led him out a side door of the gothic building (named for another insane poet) where a short time later an ambulance came to take him away. By the time they got him into the ambulance he had quieted down and didn't want to go, but they took him anyway. He was out for the rest of the term.

Needless to say, the poet's breakdown made terrific gossip among the faculty and students for several days. The conversation focused on the drama of the explosion rather than on the causes of it. Those who had been in his class became celebrities, centers of rapt attention, as they described over and over again the madman's gestures, voice, words, and facial expressions. I think the reason that they didn't talk much about the causes behind this dramatic crack-up was that most of them had been around literature long enough to assume that the threat of insanity was something that writers lived with each day. Look at Ezra Pound, Swinburne, Jones Very, Coleridge, Dr. Johnson, Christopher Smart, and William Collins. Mental imbalance was merely a fact of artistic life, something not to be questioned any more than one would question the golden leaves and hazy light of a fall afternoon. The academic poet had cracked up before, and he would do it again—at least everybody hoped he would, for the drama of it always put a little excitement into the less-than-lively existence of the students and faculty.

The students knew that the mad poet was closer to art than they were. He created it; they only studied it. Knowing that he was different from them, they felt that it was okay for him to go manifestly insane, but not for them. So what they adopted was not madness itself but parodies of it. A fellow who was in graduate school with me, a sallow, skinny twenty-six-year-old with a good mind, went to a psychiatrist at least twice a month, and more often when he could afford it. He would work all night in a hamburger joint to get money for his "treatment," which was always his priority. Everything else, tuition, books, board and room, came last. He loved to talk about his "complexes," about the "depths" he had reached while under analysis, and about the "progress" he was making.

Those of us who listened to him—in fact, he was rather interesting—were a bit doubtful about his "progress," for he never seemed to change. He was never quite well and never clinically insane, but always wandering somewhere between. During the five years we were in graduate school together, he remained always the same pale, emaciated, tortured young man.

The difference between him and his fellow-students was one of degree rather than kind. All of us had our little neuroses, and we watched over them and nursed them with the earnest solicitude of race-horse owners. We had more neuroses than psychoses because neuroses are less serious and more respectable, being psychological states in which a person still has one foot in reality. It has been said that the difference between a neurotic and a psychotic is that the neurotic sees visions and worries about his sanity, whereas the psychotic sees visions and accepts them as his reality. We wanted to be a little unbalanced but stop short of raving mania. Thus we parodied insanity. In the academic world of the arts, it was fashionable to be ever so slightly whacky; and we seemed to feel that if we could dance without paying the fiddler, why not dance?

The trouble is, more than one of us did pay the fiddler by ending up with something beyond a mere parody or imitation of madness. We were literary folk, and some of us went out of our heads. Here I come close to saying that literature actually causes insanity. Without going quite that far, I would suggest that literary art encourages mental disorders in those who may already have a propensity toward them. It cannot be entirely accidental that the incidence of mental illness is so great among people studying the arts. From what I've seen, I would say that the two most prevalent afflictions are schizophrenia and one of its major subdivisions, paranoia.

During appointments at several universities, I have met at least two dozen English professors with more-than-routine schizophrenic tendencies. I'm thinking in particular of that type of behavior that we like to call "split personality." One doesn't have to be a psychologist to see such a division in the man I'm about to describe. This fellow was in his late thirties, a specialist in the English Romantics, particularly the more emotional ones like Shelley and Keats. His problem was that he couldn't keep his hands off the coeds.

Lechery of this sort does not in itself constitute schizophrenia. To complete the picture there was the other half of him, a being which was more scornful of fleshly lust than all of the New-England Mathers put together. The puritanical side of him showed up in his lectures, for he would spend hours in the classroom "showing" the students that if they interpreted the Romantics correctly they would see that love as treated in these poets was a highly spiritual kind of thing.

True enough, the poet might use sensual imagery—as in the description of the feast in *The Eve of St. Agnes*—but such imagery was merely a means of "corporealizing" (one of his favorite words) Platonic love so as to make it clear to the reader. Then the professor would dive into a tirade against a hypothetical stupid student who construed Keats as merely driven by sex. It was not the business of poetry, the professor said, to cater to the genitalia of mankind. If indeed there were references to such things in the poetry, it was only so that the poet could describe ideal love in negatives, by telling what it was not. Poetry used sex to deny sex. Sex was base, he said; it had nothing to do with art.

In San Francisco, several years after I had left that university, I happened to run into a woman who had studied the English Romantics under the Mather-lecher schizoid I've just described. By this time she was married with two children. I had known her at the university; she was liberal, bright and friendly, so it was good to see her again. Over some drinks we talked about old times, and the conversation rather inevitably drifted onto the Mather-lecher. She mentioned something I hadn't known before—that she herself had been one of the coeds that he had made passes at. She said she had gone to his office to argue about a grade on her mid-term examination. In the course of making it clear that he wasn't going to change her "B+" to an "A−," he steadily moved his chair closer and closer to hers. He was sitting in a swivel chair with casters on it, which he pulled forward with his feet. By the time he finished telling her that he never gave "A's" to non-majors (she was in sociology), his knees were touching hers and he had both her hands in his. Then she told me an amazing thing. As though driven by some force, she leaned forward and kissed him on the mouth. For several moments they sat there like that, knees, hands and lips touching. Then suddenly the professor broke away from her; he put his head down and began to sob. "I'm sorry," he said, "I can't help it."

After our conversation, I began to mull it over, how this man could preach against sex and yet sexually approach his students (some of whom responded), only to back off and break into sobs. I had heard of hypocrites—men who talked "morality" and had adulterous affairs, etc.—but the Mather-lecher was no mere hypocrite. He was so split down the middle and so aware of it that it plunged him into fits of crying. He was laboring under a fullscale neurosis, the kind of schizophrenia that we laymen call split personality.

It's my thesis that literature helped him become what he was, but before telling about that, I'd like to tell about another victim of the arts, a student in English who in the course of his graduate training went from being a fairly normal person to a fullscale paranoid.

The graduate student—let's call him Frank—made routine progress in his Ph.D. program until he came to that great Waterloo, the comprehensive examinations. Though he felt confident, apparently he had wildly underestimated the difficulty of the exams, especially the oral part. This is an ordeal in which you go into a small seminar room with a dozen stern professors and stay for two or three hours while they ask you anything and everything about literature. It is a terrifying experience. In Frank's oral, things got off to a bad start and went downhill from there. The first question was on Rossetti and the Pre-Raphaelites, one of his weakest areas, and Frank fielded it poorly, so that his confidence was shattered right from the beginning. After that, he was so shaken that he couldn't even handle questions in his specialty, the Elizabethans. He didn't know Greville from Gascoigne from Gorboduc, and after only ten or fifteen minutes it was apparent to everyone that a disaster had occurred.

Anyone who has gone through the Ph.D. grind knows the procedure of the oral exam: after they question you they send you out of the room while they decide your fate. You know how it feels to stand there in the hallway while they deliberate over the dissected corpse of your intellect. The minutes creep like snails while in your mind the mistakes you made magnify themselves into huge chimeras of failure. But in most cases, when the door finally opens, there is good news in the form of a file of smiling professors who shake your hand and congratulate you.

In Frank's case, however, the professors wore grim expressions, and the exam chairman had to tell him what he was already sure of, that he had failed. Moreover, the examiners felt it their duty to inform him he might never pass unless he showed vast improvement. It was a heavy blow, and from that moment Frank began to show paranoid behavior. He told me later that day that the examiners had conspired against him, intentionally asking him trick questions to throw him off. I was pretty sure this wasn't true, though I tried to be sympathetic with him.

Later on, though, as his paranoia grew, I got tired of listening to his tales of persecution. For one thing, they were getting a little too wild, like the one he told me about going to see his adviser. He claimed that the adviser had hidden a television camera behind some bookcases to witness everything Frank was saying. I asked him if he had actually seen it, and he answered no, but he knew it was there behind those bookcases. When I told him I thought he was imagining things, he began to accuse me of helping the graduate school to conspire against him in order to stop him from getting his doctorate. I got sore and told him he was crazy. That was the end of our friendship.

It's entirely possible that Frank would have become a paranoid even if he had never been exposed to literature, just as the schizophrenic Mather-lecher might have been what he was, with or without the great books. All I can say is that I doubt it and go on to offer some reasons why I feel this way.

I think literature encourages schizophrenia and paranoia. It encourages schizophrenia by enticing those who study and teach it to live in two different worlds at the same time, that of fiction and that of reality. The significance of such a split existence can best be seen by contrasting life in the "humanities" with life in other academic disciplines. Suppose you are a professor of engineering, forestry, or chemistry. You can see that the technical matter you study and teach has no close resemblance to your life outside the classroom and library. Topics like bridges, trees, or sodium nitrate make no threat to imitate large parts of our lives.

But when we turn to the arts, our subject matter is purportedly man's life, all of it; and we judge artists on how well they imitate, literally or symbolically, the reality in which we live. Our subject matter tries to be us, but it never can; all it can do is divide us between itself and ourselves. This problem doesn't arise in social sciences like anthropology, history or sociology because in these disciplines the subject matter is actual life, real cultures and societies, so that professors in these fields are studying and teaching something that is fundamentally a part of themselves.

In technology and "hard" science, the subject matter is *distinct* from our lives; in social science it *is* our lives; but in the arts it is an *imitation* of our lives. If we become too involved in the beautiful imitation, we can begin to lose touch with the real thing. We may end up living in two different worlds, which is uncomfortable if not dangerous. Of course, one can find madness in any discipline, from anthropology to zoology; but nowhere is it made so attractive as in the world of the arts, which seems to have more crazy people than any other field.

If the influence of the great books can cleave our personalities in two, it can also move us toward paranoia. It is worth noticing that in virtually every famous story the hero is seriously threatened by something; something is after him, out to get him, and he must act or perish. The persecuted hero takes many forms, ranging from the epic to the absurd. Just as Odysseus is convinced that the suitors are out to get his wife and property away from him, so is the hero of Camus' *The Stranger* convinced that the existential meaninglessness of the cosmos is out to get him.

Perhaps the most lengthy roster of persecuted heroes is to be found in English literature. It is hard to find characters more hunted and haunted, and more aware of it, than Beowulf, Everyman, Malory's Lancelot, Spenser's Red Cross Knight, Hamlet, Othello, Milton's Satan, Bunyan's Christian, Richardson's Clarissa, Scott's Ivanhoe, Coleridge's Ancient Mariner, Dickens's Oliver Twist, Hardy's Tess, Eliot's Prufrock, and Amis's Lucky Jim. What all of these famous characters have in common is the certain knowledge that something or somebody is out to get them. However, we have to stop short of calling them paranoids, because as their stories unfold we learn that the evil they face is quite real, whether it is a physical presence like Beowulf's Grendel or an abstraction like Lucky Jim's Academe. On the other hand, in actual paranoia the persecuting forces are imaginary or illusory.

If the famous heroes are not technically paranoid, how can they encourage paranoia in those who study them? The answer lies in the nature of artistic narrative. To capture and maintain the audience's interest, there seems to be no other way than to place the emphasis on the hero's reaction to the threat rather than on the threat itself. For example, we are more interested in Satan's schemes than in God's opposition to him; more interested in Hamlet's pale cast of thought than in the murder which made him think; more interested in Everyman's struggle for salvation than in the fact of death, which caused that struggle. We respond to the persecution, not the persecutor. As the authors of the four Gospels must have known, it is persecution that makes the greatest art. Neither on Herod nor on Pilate but on Christ is where the artistic accent must fall. If we devote our careers to studying the rhetoric of persecution, we may begin to feel that something is out to get us.

As a kind of footnote to the foregoing remarks about literature, schizophrenia, and paranoia, it should be mentioned that many of the most beautiful and powerful passages in literature are about insanity. Perhaps the best of all are in Shakespeare. Who could forget the sweet bells jangled in the minds of Hamlet and Ophelia, the ravings of Othello, or the damned spot of Lady Macbeth? Sometimes a second-rate poet is remembered chiefly because he wrote one good poem about madness, as in George Crabbe's *Peter Grimes*, which was eventually made into a fine opera. The success of mental imbalance as a literary theme is partly due to the old custom of seeing the poet as a fascinating madman, a tradition reaching as far back as Plato. But usually the poet's insanity has been looked upon as a great virtue, a fine frenzy which is a sine qua non for the creation of major works of art.

I think it would pay us to stop looking on madness as valuable and fashionable. We need to clear our heads long enough to investigate the possibility that literature can encourage mental imbalance in those who live with it too long.

Section 2

Getting Hung Up on the Past

Discuss the relationship between man and the past, the meaning of history and man's relationship to it, as defined and examined in the works of four of the following writers: Joyce, Yeats, Eliot, Pound, Faulkner, Warren, Bellow. Include in your essay specific discussion of at least one work by each writer you choose. How does the significance of history and the past, or, in some cases, the attempt to discover that significance, help not only to define the human condition within the work, but also the form of the work? Try to move beyond such generalizations as, "the past was wonderful and the present is awful."

—Question used on an examination for the Master of Arts in English

I used to teach with a man who had been fired from a major university. Although for years he was extremely bitter about it, it could be argued that because it happens frequently, there is nothing to be ashamed of in being let go from a big school. It's the practice of many front-rank universities to hire several assistant professors when there is room on the tenured staff for only one. The idea is to let the young faculty members fight it out, until, after several years, the best person emerges. This system is supposed to ensure that the university retains only the outstanding people on its permanent faculty. Most of the people who are dismissed by the big schools are not terribly shocked or traumatized by the experience. They know that in the academic rat race you pay your money and you take your chance. They usually make good careers for themselves at lesser but respectable universities or at decent state colleges. Moreover, many of them do well financially. As high men at state colleges they are often paid more than they presumably would have gotten as low men at the prestigious universities.

I hope that what I've just said doesn't imply that I'm defending the system. I'm not. I think it's brutal, and because it tends to be subjective and emotional, it doesn't guarantee quality. All I'm saying is that most of those victimized by the system make a pretty good recovery. They manage to forget the past, to live down the humiliation of being told, in so many words, that they're inadequate or incompetent and that the decade they've invested in getting the Ph.D. and getting ready for life at a major university was a waste of time.

Usually when the department chairman calls a person in to tell him he's fired, he tries to soften the blow by saying that there is a real need "for good men like you" at the state colleges and small universities, and that it is "really for your own good" that this action is being taken. Often the chairman feels embarrassed or guilty enough to offer to write a strong letter of recommendation or to try in some other way to get the unfortunate fellow a job elsewhere. This is what happened to the man I used to teach with. His former chairman had gone all out to get him the very best state college job available. And in fact it was a good job—a light teaching load, a good location, and ten thousand a year, which at that time was high pay for an assistant professor. Also, the students were bright and the school offered several in-depth courses in my colleague's field, which was the Victorians. But none of this was any consolation to my colleague. He could never get off the theme of his unfortunate fall from a major university, and he used to bore us during coffee breaks with tedious tales of the spilt milk of his career. It got so bad that people began to avoid him.

One day a well-meaning anthropologist on our faculty suggested to him that it was unhealthy to go on dwelling on the past, the unrelivable past. "Pull up your socks," he said, "and get on with the more important tasks of today and the future. You'll feel a lot better if you do." But my colleague ignored this advice. It was clear that he had no intention of swerving from his vocation of lamenting the past. Eventually word got around that he was boring not only his colleagues but also his students with his favorite theme. When the student ratings of faculty came out (this was the first year we had them at that school), we saw that he had been crucified. Using actual quotations from the students, the rating-book described him as "dull as hell" and, quite accurately, "too hung up on the past." However, the Man of the Past (which I'll call him from now on) wasn't hurt by the failing ratings handed him by his students. He didn't care what they said because he was so trapped in the past that nothing could get to him. His fixation on years gone by was an impervious armor through which nothing, not even common sense, could penetrate.

In those rare moments when the Man of the Past wasn't boring his classes with his personal sorrows, he lectured on Victorian literature. He was particularly fascinated, even though his students weren't, with the oppressive nostalgia that bulks large in so many writers of nineteenth-century England. He liked to talk about *In Memoriam*—about the death of Tennyson's friend Hallam and how the poet could never get over it. The Man of the Past's favorite passage was Stanza VII, the one beginning "Dark house, by which once more I stand." He liked to recite it to his yawning class in a deep dramatic voice:

> Dark house, by which once more I stand
>> Here in the long unlovely street,
>> Doors where my heart was used to beat
> So quickly, waiting for a hand,
> A hand that can be clasp'd no more—
>> Behold me, for I cannot sleep,
>> And like a guilty thing I creep
> At earliest morning to the door.
> He is not here; but far away
>> The noise of life begins again,
>> And ghastly through the drizzling rain
> On the bald street breaks the blank day.

Sometimes, when the weight of years gone by sat with more than usual cumbrousness on the shoulders of the Man of the Past, tears would steal into his pale eyes as he recited Tennyson, and the students would be embarrassed and fidgety in their seats. They liked it better when he talked about things they thought were funny, like the Queen's blind and steadfast refusal to accept the death of her beloved Prince Albert, though these were very serious things to the Man of the Past. The Victorian age was nostalgic, and it fed and nurtured his own nostalgia. It was all very symbiotic: the nineteenth century needed professors like him to keep it alive, and he needed the nineteenth century as a means of extending on a broad scale his fixation on the past.

It can't be said that literature by itself transformed a sane man into a foolish, self-destructive and boring fellow like the Man of the Past. But it helped. People in the "humanities" usually have a hard time getting over things. Though the Man of the Past was an extreme case, I think he effectively symbolizes the tendency among those who teach and study art to spend too much of their energies upon the unchangeable and over-and-done-with past. A brief look at a few of the great books can show us how literature can bog us down fruitlessly in yesteryear.

The great books are characteristically heavy with nostalgia. Though the Victorians excel in this area, writers of all periods of literature have an excessive reverence and yearning for the past. No era in English literature is free from nostalgia for some previous literary or cultural period. Even in the beginning, in such poems as *Beowulf* or *The Wanderer*, there is a kind of wistful yearning for an older or simpler time when every warrior had his secure spot in the mead-hall and knew precisely where he stood in the still-intact feudal system. The Middle English writers looked back with equal yearning on an age of chivalry and courtly love which had vanished centuries before they wrote about it. Similarly, the Renaissance and "Augustan" or "Neoclassical" age longed for an irretrievable Golden Age of ancient Rome. The Romantics loved the Greeks (as in Shelley's *Prometheus Unbound* or Keats' *Ode on a Grecian Urn*), but what they loved even more was the medieval period, which they revived again and again. Some of the better efforts were Scott's *Ivanhoe*, Keats' *La Belle Dame Sans Merci*, and Coleridge's *Christabel*.

The medieval revival continued strongly into Victoria's reign, refusing to be supplanted until the literary declaration of independence by early twentieth-century writers like T. E. Hulme and T. S. Eliot. But the rebels tended to replace one nostalgia with another, instead of actually bringing in something new. Discarding the pseudomedievalism and the arrested Romanticism of the nineteenth century, they brought in what they thought was an entirely new species of neoclassicism. Yet with a great sameness every age is a neoclassical age, for each literary generation, however much it rebels against the one before it, is in love with some large section of the past, to which it looks for standards, guidance, rules, and procedure.

Thus it seems impossible to read the great books without automatically beginning to share the musty nostalgia that permeates their pages. Even when we are reading something that seems "strictly contemporary to its time," which is how one of my teachers described *Tom Jones*, we are reading nostalgia. For Fielding skillfully guides the artistry of his narrative according to precepts and attitudes established in practice and theory by writers of the classical times in which Fielding was deeply and broadly educated. And Fielding's view of man, though essentially that of his time, also owed something to the ideals, attitudes, and insights which he had gleaned from his readings in a good many ancient Roman authors, with Virgil and Horace being probably the most important.

Because most good writers are thoroughly steeped in the literature that came before them, they can never, even if they wish to, sever themselves from the past. As Samuel Butler said, "The history of art is the history of revivals." (The nineteenth-century Butler, quoted from his *Note Books*.) Alain Robbe-Grillet, exponent of the French "new novel," tried to do something utterly new but did so only stylistically. As far as the content or plots of his stories are concerned, he is frequently very old fashioned, as in the hackneyed love triangles of *Jealousy* or *Last Year at Marienbad*, triangles that remind us of the earliest stories ever told.

The nostalgia which is an integral part of any novel, play, or poem is a manifestation of the truism that in the world of the creative writer there is surprisingly little that is new under the sun, a situation which is underscored by the continuous efforts of scholars to show that whatever an author uses has been used before.

I have suggested that literary art, because it is built on earlier literatures or cultures, is inherently nostalgic in its subject matter or style or both. Another way that literature partakes in nostalgia is by bringing to its reader, in a highly interesting way, a living past. I say "living" because in nonliterary approaches to the past like history or archaeology, former times are recognized as concluded, and there is no effort in these disciplines to give people the illusion that things are still going on. We read Tennyson, Fielding, or Virgil not because they are dead and done with but because they can make the past live again in a very powerful way. As teachers of the great books, we fetch back the past each day, until it's utterly routine for us to live with one foot in the snows of yesteryear and the other in the fires of today. It's no wonder that our view of reality is sometimes a little warped. If we are criticized for overemphasizing the years gone by and neglecting the present, we usually snap back at our critics with the idea that there can be no understanding the present without knowing the past. We may even rap out a provocative aphorism: "Those who are ignorant of the past are condemned to relive it."

For many years I fervently believed that aphorism. Then one day I abruptly abandoned it. I guess my intellectual opposition to it had been building in my subconscious for a long time, because when it finally let go, it let go with considerable force. It happened this way. The first time I visited the campus of a large midwestern university (it was winter), I happened to notice an inscription high over the entrance to the main library: "He who knows only his own times remains always a child." It was chiseled in large, blockish letters, very authoritative looking. My instant reaction to it was anger. Not only did it beg the question of what's wrong with being a "child," it also seemed somehow to sneer down at me that I had better get going if I were ever to count myself among the real adults, those who because they thoroughly knew the past were grown up enough to help dictate the shaping of the future and to help bring about the salvation of mankind.

As I stood there in the dirty, week-old snow, looking up at those hortatory words, I became so angry that I didn't even notice the subfreezing temperature, until finally my hands and feet, by growing numb, tugged me back into the reality of the present moment. I trudged away and spent most of that pale afternoon thinking about how wrong our pompous pronouncements on the past had been. I thought about the thousands of heartless rulers and nasty little politicians of history and how nearly every one of them from Herod to Hitler had used some kind of resuscitation of the past to suppress, torture, or murder his fellow human beings.

I realized that it was not only power that corrupted. It was also the knowledge of the past, for the possession of such knowledge was one of the chief avenues to power. The more one knows about what has happened, the more one can make things happen. This is real power; of course it corrupts. I also thought about how psychologically unhealthy it is to dwell on the past; how futile and frustrating it is to try to dam up and get back the water under the bridge; how people have wasted careers or entire lives in the folly of over-remembering. I promised myself that I would stop telling my students that by intensively studying literature, that gorgeous preservation of the past, they could easily understand the present and the future.

I decided to tell them instead that all they really needed for the survival of themselves and their fellow men was a slightly-better-than-nodding acquaintance with the records and documents of the past, not the utter saturation that literature seemed to demand. I decided to tell them that the avenue to virtue and wisdom lay not through the deep woods of the great books but more probably through the sunny fields of common sense and concern for others. I decided to propound to them the thesis that more than a few villains had ridden to tyranny on the shoulders of their masterful knowledge of the past, and that most of them remained as blind and insensitive as the thickest, darkest night. I decided to suggest to them that the aphorism be revised to read "Those who know the past are condemned to relive it and take a lot of innocent people along with them." I decided to tell them to beware of being sucked into the fetching rhetoric of the great heroes of literature who are hung up on the past and refuse to let it go even if it means their own destruction; I mean the soreheads or brooders like Achilles, Antigone, Dante, Don Quixote, Hamlet, Hester Prynne, and many, many others. And finally I decided to warn them about that inscription over the library door. For it demanded excessive knowledge of the past, not merely a casual acquaintance with it. That is what it had to mean; why else put it over the lintel of a million-volume library?

Later that day I went back to the library and threw a snowball at the inscription over the door. Then, as I stood there looking up at the splatted remnants of my snowball, my anger began to subside. I had gotten something out of my system. Perhaps I would not after all lecture so fervently to my students on the evils of over-knowing the past. But as I walked away from the library I also knew that never again would the past be all important.

Section 3

Traveling in the Realms of Gold: Does Literature Make Us Materialistic?

Deep in our hearts, wealth is the holiest thing.
—Juvenal, The First Satire

About five years ago, I was invited to dinner at the home of one of my colleagues, a fellow I had often seen on campus but didn't really know very well. He seemed to be a pleasant person, almost too pleasant. He and his wife were rumored to have a very expensive house, and I was looking forward to seeing it.

When I got there, I saw that the rumors were true. It was a gigantic, glassy A-frame, with its feet in the pines and a wide view of the mountains. The interior was a delightful maze of cantilevers, balconies and catwalks, all done up in a variety of natural finish woods—cedar, oak, pine, and walnut. The furniture had a theme of teak and black leather or vinyl, and there were many expensive looking paintings and sculptures throughout the house, as I learned on the seventy-five-cent tour given me by my colleague, during which time he kept telling me how much everything had cost.

As I was being guided through the opulent beauty of this home, the question that kept running through my mind was "How can they afford it on a professor's skinny salary?" I was later to learn that they couldn't, and that they maintained their living style by both husband and wife working and by being constantly in debt. I eventually got to know them well

93

enough to know that in spite of their public smiles they were pretty unhappy amid all that pelf.

That same year I was invited to the home of another colleague, one who was rumored to live in a very impoverished style. Again the rumors proved to be correct. His house was a tiny crackerbox badly in need of a paint job and some lawn work, though even if the place had been fixed up, it still would have looked rather cheap. There was no TV aerial. Several gaunt children stood in the yard. My hosts didn't offer to give me a tour of their house, but there probably wasn't much to see anyway. As I ate spaghetti from the plastic dishes and conversed with them, I wondered why they chose to live in such a substandard way. Surely his salary, though meager, could go farther than this.

What I finally learned, through the conversation that night and through gossip I heard later, was that although they could well afford it (she had a substantial annuity), they felt less materialistic and less guilty if they denied themselves the affluence so easily available in modern American society. They were long-faced and always too serious, and they seemed almost to take pleasure in being unhappy and perpetually going without.

I used to spend a lot of time comparing these two colleagues, the A-framer and the Crackerboxer. It seemed clear that although they lived at opposite ends of the lifestyle spectrum, they had something in common: they both had a warped or unbalanced sense of money, goods, and luxury. One was too materialistic and the other not enough. After comparing them with the rest of the department, it occurred to me that these two differed only in degree, not in kind, from their colleagues. I hadn't noticed it before, but now I could see that all of us, certainly including myself, had a distorted sense of the material side of life. It was just that we didn't go quite as far as the A-framer or the Crackerboxer. Yet sure enough, if you looked closely at us, you could see that all of us were warped, that all of us had either an overdeveloped or underdeveloped concern with money and things like that. One of us wore a different twenty-dollar shirt every day and another never changed his. One of us drove a Cadillac and the other one walked. All of us were unhappy, and one cause of it was that we could never seem to get comfortable with the affluence that the modern world dumps on us. Maybe we were born with a tendency toward this unhappiness with the material world, but it's possible that our studies of literature pushed us farther along the way.

If the great books can encourage us to be unbalanced materialistically, one way they do it is through the imagery or metaphor of riches. Everyone knows Shakespeare's famous description of Cleopatra's barge:

> The barge she sat in, like a burnish'd throne,
> Burned on the water. The poop was beaten gold;
> Purple the sails, and so perfumed that
> The winds were love-sick with them. The oars were silver,
> Which to the tune of flutes kept stroke, and made
> The water which they beat to follow faster,
> As amorous of their strokes. For her own person,
> It beggar'd all description: she did lie
> In her pavilion—cloth-of-gold of tissue—
> O'er picturing that Venus where we see
> The fancy outwork nature.

Enobarbus, the character who gives the description, is somewhat of a teller of tall tales, and Cleopatra's barge might not have been quite this luxurious. Even so, generations of readers have been impressed with the sheer richness of the description, regardless of whether it's accurate or what it may symbolize.

It's interesting to note how many of the famous passages in Shakespeare are literally or figuratively about material luxury or wealth. "Costly thy habit as thy purse can buy,/ But not expressed in fancy; rich, not gaudy." "Now all the youth of England are on fire,/ And silken dalliance in the wardrobe lies." "Bell, book, and candle shall not drive me back,/ When gold and silver becks me to come on." "All the perfumes of Arabia will not sweeten this little hand." "My daughter! My ducats!" "Who steals my purse steals trash." "This royal throne of kinds, this scepter'd isle." "It seems she hangs upon the cheek of night/ Like a rich jewel in an Ethiop's ear." "Those are pearls that were his eyes."

These renowned lines from various plays speak in favor of riches ("costly thy habit") and against riches ("who steals my purse"). But all the lines have in common a clever use of an image of wealth or luxury. Indeed, Shakespeare's use of the figure of riches is so powerful that we tend to forget what kind of value he originally assigned to the figure, good or bad. As the poetry of the famous passages rests comfortably in our literary memory, there is a gradual withering away of the original meaning, so that we retain only the concrete image of riches itself.

I believe that one reason people like to read is that they enjoy the constant references that great writers make to money, gold, jewels, or other luxuries. Whether the author is damning or praising material opulence, his eloquent and artistic references to opulence are extremely palatable to most readers. Even a devout Christian can enjoy the flashy gold of Milton's Pandemonium, although Pandemonium is Satan's palace:

Anon out of the earth a fabric huge
Rose like an exhalation, with the sound
Of dulcet symphonies and voices sweet,
Built like a temple, where pilasters round
Were set, and Doric pillars overlaid
With golden architrave; nor did there want
Cornice or frieze, with bossy sculptures graven;
The roof was fretted gold. Not Babylon
Nor great Alcairo such magnificence
Equaled in all their glories to enshrine
Belus or Serapis their gods, or seat
Their kings, when Egypt with Assyria strove
In wealth and luxury.

On the other hand, a strict atheist can enjoy the riches of heaven as they are beautifully described by most poets. The use of riches or luxuries as metaphor or imagery is standard and widespread throughout the literature of the Western World, from the Song of Solomon to *Gone with the Wind,* from the *Odyssey* to *The Wasteland.* To read heavily in the great books is to undergo repeated exposure to the infinite riches in the little rooms of the creative imagination. I think that the person who spends his career this way is much more prone than the average man to feel an anxiety towards the presence of whatever material wealth he finds in his daily life. Thus he characteristically has trouble responding; he either over- or underreacts. Whether he is tweedy or seedy, an A-framer or a Crackerboxer, we can see that he has failed to make a balanced and harmonious adjustment to riches or luxury. Whether he lives way up high or way down low on the hog, he reveals that he has an excessive and unhealthy concern with wealth, aggravated each day by the overwhelming presence of the imagery of riches in the great books.

The appeal of the imagery of riches is strengthened by literature's constant exploitation of our senses. Good writers spend many words telling us not only how things looked, but also how they felt, sounded, tasted, or smelled. When we say of an author that he is "sensuous," we usually mean that he's a successful artist. Among the most sensuous in English literature are Chaucer, Spenser, Shakespeare, Donne, Bunyan, Pope, Blake, Keats, Tennyson, and Dylan Thomas. One effect of such writers on us is to open up our senses and make us more aware of the presence of physical things around us. It would seem to follow that the more aware we are of physical things, the more we are going to be interested in them. An increased interest in things could result in a greater acquisitiveness or even an inordinate fear of acquisitiveness. It's possible that the "heightened awareness" granted to us by the great books could induce a heightened materialism, which contributes to the unbalanced response to money and luxury so common among professors.

There is an irony in the way that literature tries to cater to our spiritual life and at the same time rubs our noses too much in the gross materialism of the world, until we simply don't know how to react to the getting and spending part of life. This paradox in the great books can be symbolized by the third from the last paragraph in Bunyan's *Pilgrim's Progress*, which gives the reader a very materialistic glimpse into the Celestial City:

> Now just as the gates were opened to let in the men, I looked in after them, and, behold, the City shone like the sun; the streets also were paved with gold, and in them walked many men, with crowns on their heads, palms in their hands, and golden harps to sing praises withal.

Section 4

Being Naive about Ingratitude

And one of them, when he saw that he was healed, turned back, and with a loud voice glorified God, and fell down on his face at his feet, giving him thanks: and he was a Samaritan. And Jesus answering said, Were there not ten cleansed? but where are the nine?
— *The Gospel According to Luke xvii. 15-17*

It's not unusual for a college professor to feel a bit depressed at the end of spring term. We know that old feeling of "another year gone and not much to show for it." Last spring a colleague of mine had it bad. He was depressed, he told me, because although he had worked hard at teaching his English literature classes, no one ever thanked him. He said it was the same every term: the kids would come to class, listen politely, take notes, participate in class discussion, do reasonably well on the tests, and then after the final examination they'd walk out the door without saying a word, never to be seen again.

In fact, my colleague had a reputation as one of the better teachers on the campus. He was articulate, engaging, and well informed. He knew he was doing a good job, too. It was just that no one, no student, no fellow professor, no administrator, ever seemed to give him a single word of appreciation. To be accurate, however, it should be mentioned that two or three times each year he could have sworn he heard a murmured "thank you" or "great course" or "enjoyed it" as the students filed out of the final exam. But that might have been all in his mind; and even if it weren't, it wasn't enough to overcome his conviction that his world was seething with ingratitude. What was the use of knocking yourself out if no one ever thanked you? Then my colleague would plunge into a dissertation on ingratitude, waving his arms in the air as he damned the ingrate students, faculty, administration, and public, to all of whom he was giving his precious time and energies for a piddling salary and no fringe benefits.

I'm not sure what I should do to help my colleague. Perhaps I should introduce him to an old friend of mine, an accountant. My friend has a secure and high paying job, a pleasant wife, and a beautiful new home plus all the accoutrements of the "good life," such as two cars, a sailboat, and plenty of skiing and hiking equipment. He is the kind of fellow who at first glance seems on top of the world. But he has a burden. The cross he bears is a son, now about twelve years old, who is mentally retarded. It would be an understatement to say that he cramps his father's style. My friend is active and athletic, an avid mountain climber and skier. But because it is impossible for his son to do these things, and because he is a genuine family man, he must severely limit himself. Though he finds this frustrating, he does it anyway. And he never complains. To the end of his days he will be saddled with that handicapped son whom he willingly and cheerfully cares for with all of his energy and attention. In the boy's infant years he spent a fortune on tests and therapy for him, and the special schools and nurses will cost another fortune before the story is done. He says he can afford it, so he doesn't mind, even though his son will never be able to say a single word of thanks to him. Nor does my friend imitate the whinings of many a writer, teacher, or fictional hero. He doesn't expect God or anybody to rush to praise him merely because he took up his burden.

Though it's true that the accountant's situation is not the same as that of my unhappy colleague on the campus, perhaps I should introduce them to each other. Then maybe the professor could learn a lesson that is seldom taught in the great works of English literature: *There are few things more natural than ingratitude.* No matter how virtuous we are and how well we do our job, the world is liable to give us small thanks for it. Therefore it is naive, and psychologically damaging, for us to work ourselves into a sweat over the essential thanklessness of life.

But the famous poets, novelists and dramatists are enormously naive about ingratitude. There seems to be something in the very nature of literature that prevents writers from being any other way. Fictional characters are either rewarded or not rewarded, but in either case the author is forced to deal with the subject of reward. To deal with it is invariably to get onto the topic of gratitude. To treat gratitude artistically is to lay upon it more stress than it ought to receive in our lives. Here is another limitation or shortcoming of literary art: because it cannot be anything other than heightened or emphatic language, it tends to emphasize whatever subject the artist applies it to. Because gratitude—or ingratitude—is a significant part of virtually any literary work which involves action, the reader is forced to make a sizeable space for it in his mind. If he is a heavy reader, there is every chance that he will become inordinately concerned with gratitude and that he will make the mistake of assuming that other people should be as aware of gratitude as he is. Then, like the bruised and sensitive authors he has been reading, he will go about in perpetual disillusionment at the not very astonishing fact that the world is a thankless place.

The persistence of the theme of gratitude in literature can be suggested by looking at some recurring types of plots. We can begin by pointing to the familiar situation in which the hero performs a service and is rewarded for it by a grateful god, ruler, or other person of power. In the literature of the Western World there are literally thousands of notable writings that fit this pattern, ranging from Old Testament stories like those of Abraham, Joseph, or Ruth to modern novels like *Humphry Clinker* or *Jane Eyre*. Between the Old Testament and the modern novel are hundreds of reward-winners like Odysseus, Aeneis, and Beowulf. Even when the hero is made to look absurd and made to receive absurd rewards, as in *Don Quixote* or *Hudibras*, the author is forced to deal with some kind of reward; there is no avoiding it either in heroic or mock heroic action.

Nor can it be avoided in the tragic kind of narrative. The thing that appalls us in the stories of Oedipus Rex, Romeo and Juliet, or Daisy Miller is that these decent persons are treated so unfairly by gods, parents, or snobbish Europeans. Powerful tragedies often leave us with the feeling that the world owed the hero a living and failed to deliver it. Such a world reeks of ingratitude in that it has failed to recognize and recompense the essential goodness in the hero's character. If the tragic hero himself is evil, like Richard the Third or the Jew of Malta, then we feel that it is he, instead of the world, who has failed to show gratitude for the essential goodness that can be found in his immediate environment. Whether the heroes of tragedy are good or bad, they are always misaligned with the worlds they live in; and the misalignment can usually be expressed in terms of gratitude or ingratitude.

In more "realistic" literature, like the naturalistic novels of the Goncourts, Zola, Hardy, Gissing, Crane and Norris, the implication seems to be that a conspiracy of cosmological and sociological forces has doomed a guiltless hero. Because the forces are portrayed as unconscious and thus amoral, the issue of gratitude would seem irrelevant. But we read as human beings, and it is probably impossible for us to think of abstract forces without anthropomorphizing them. And once we have personified the abstract, we can get angry at it and feel a sense of outrage at the profound ingratitude of the universe and society.

Roughly speaking, narrative writers of all ages have restricted themselves to two categories of plot. One bestows rewards and the other takes them away. Inescapably, both involve gratitude. The same can be said of lyric poets of all periods. Though they tell no stories as such, they stress gratitude; for it has always been a central function of poetry either to give thanks or ask for thanks. Ancients like Pindar and Horace have grateful praise for heroes and fatherland; other ancients like Sappho and Catullus ask for gratitude from their lovers. Louder in their demands for gratitude are satirists like Persius and Juvenal. Needless to say, the giving and taking of credit, thanks, and gratitude is to this day a prime concern of the lyrical poet.

From what I've seen, I would say that English literature has an unusually strong preoccupation with gratitude—or ingratitude. Some of the finest narrative works owe a good part of their conception to a sense of indignation at the heights to which ingratitude can soar. Probably the most famous is the "filial ingratitude" that King Lear rants about. Then there is *Paradise Lost,* with its double ingratitude of Satan and Adam in rebellion against the God that created them. In the next century Gulliver is delighted to learn that ingratitude is a "capital crime" in Lilliput. In the quandaries of Pip in *Great Expectations,* the Victorian age produced a masterful study of the problems of gratitude, and perhaps the best twentieth-century exploration of the theme is *Ulysses,* in which so few people are grateful for the gentle decencies of Leopold Bloom. In a similar vein, the greatest English lyrical poems are essentially demands for appreciation of speaker or subject: Caedmon's *Hymn, Alysoun, Sonnet 73* ("That time of year thou mayest in me behold"), *Lycidas, Adonais, Ode on a Grecian Urn,* and *Among School Children.* Hardly any English writer seems to know that gratitude is no good when you have to ask for it.

Literature is a kind of coin with gratitude on one side and ingratitude on the other. Whichever side the writer emphasizes, he has the effect of making those who read too much slightly paranoid about the debts they think society owes them. Insofar as my colleague with the spring-term blues is a learned and enthusiastic teacher of English literature, he is a fool about gratitude. Perhaps it would help him if I were to introduce him to the well-adjusted accountant. But I don't know. The accountant is not an especially verbal man and he might not be able to explain things.

Section 5

How to Get Ulcers from the Great Books

Chicken Little was right.

—*graffito in a restroom*

Any competent physician or psychologist will tell you that worrying can be bad for you. We know that some worry is necessary to motivate us to get the job done, but carried to excess it can destroy our morale, our health, our bank accounts, and our whole way of life. Graduate students worry a great deal, especially in the arts. Worrying almost ruined me when I was pursuing my Ph.D. During the year before my comprehensive doctoral examinations, I worried so fiercely that I lost thirty pounds and started to develop a duodenal ulcer. My wife urged me to see a doctor but I was afraid he would put me in the hospital, delaying my examinations. I would have to prepare all over again, and I couldn't stand that. I swore that I would take those examinations even if I had to be carried into them on a stretcher. As it turned out, I was able to walk into them.

After the examinations, my stomach was better and I got some of my weight back. Some of my professors seemed pleased to see that I had been so willing to risk my health for the sake of English literature. Here was a man, they thought, who really gave a damn. And I was delighted that they were pleased with me. I must have been out of my mind to feel that way. Now, years later and not a whole lot wiser, I nevertheless know that my innards are worth more than the study of English literature.

To blame our ulcers on the "system" of the Ph.D. program is to stop

103

short of the actual cause. One real culprit is art itself, for a successful work of art is an eloquent display of anxious concern. In deciding whether a novel, poem or play is good, we demand that the writer somehow convey to us his deep and strenuous commitment to his subject. He may love or hate his subject, but in either case we insist that he care about it. If he doesn't, his writing tends to strike us as superficial, insincere, and "journalistic"—epithets we use on best-sellers or freshman English papers.

The differences between *care*, or *concern*, and *worry* are slight. Other synonyms belonging to this group are *distress, uneasiness,* and *anxiety.* A good author exhibits all of these toward his subject. He characteristically overreacts to situations, and when his overreaction is drastic and extreme, he has a chance of producing a great work. It's no exaggeration to say that without *care, concern* or *anxiety*—in short, without *worry*— art could not exist. And woe unto the artist who, however sincere, gives even the impression of not caring. At the grand opening of the John F. Kennedy Center for the Performing Arts, a number of people criticized Leonard Bernstein's original *Mass,* which he had written and performed for the occasion. The most devastating comment came from a Jesuit intellectual who said that Bernstein (who is Jewish) had no actual *concern* for the Christian ritual of mass. It would not be changing things much to say that, according to the Jesuit, Bernstein did not sufficiently *worry* about his material.

It seems reasonable to assume that if we devote much of our time to studying the arts, we run the risk of acquiring the worry habit. The human tendency is to imitate that which we are constantly exposed to. In our "profession" we spend hours each day with some of the most consummate and articulate worriers who ever trod the earth's imagined corners: Shakespeare, Donne, Milton, Dr. Johnson, Blake, Wordsworth, Tennyson, Hardy, Yeats, and many more. There is probably no escape from their influence. Nor is it any surprise that English departments seem to be heavily staffed with worry warts.

I remember in particular one Shakespeare scholar, a woman with a querulous tremolo of a voice. Her constant theme was that the sky was falling—that we'd never survive on our budget, that the undergraduates might cheat, that the graduate students might unionize, that the library might go broke, and so on. Now as I think back on those meetings, I feel that her literary studies helped her become what she was. For probably no man who ever took pen in hand cared—or worried—more about his material than Shakespeare. It is his almost fanatical concern for his art that provides him, ironically, with the effortless grace and the easy brilliance that enchant us.

But what are we enchanted into? Perhaps it is the acceptance of the tall haggard spectre of worry. To go near the Bard of Avon is to be infected with his gorgeous anxieties. It's interesting to note how many of his memorable passages are exercises in worrying. Speeches like "To be or not to be" are such stuff as ulcers are made on, regular manuals of instruction in the destructive art of worrying. The list of distinguished worriers in Shakespeare's tragedies is a lengthy one, including such heavyweights as Richard the Second, Brutus, Othello, Lear, Macbeth, and, above all, Hamlet. Generally speaking, the fame of the play increases in direct proportion to the amount of worrying it contains. The same is true of most of the literature of the Western World.

The menace of worrying is built into literature just as it is built into the English language. It seems grimly appropriate that the word *worry* derives from the Anglo-Saxon *wyrgan,* meaning "to strangle."

Part IV

Four Ways to Decrease Our Mental Powers

Section 1

The
Misuse
of
Opinion

How long halt ye between two opinions?
—I Kings xviii. 21

One of Chekhov's most powerful stories is *The Darling*. It's a brief tale about a young woman who was so sweet that everyone called her "The Darling." But beneath that sweet surface she struggled with a severe problem. The trouble was, she didn't have any opinions on anything. She felt a great anxiety at this vacuum inside of her, and as a result she went around looking desperately for opinions to have. She wasn't particular; just about any opinion would do, as long as it was one that she could say with force and conviction, as if it were the product of deep thought and strong feeling. This way she could not only get away from the vacuum inside herself but also have the dignity and status that seemed to go along with taking a stand and having something definite to say.

The first time I read the story I was an undergraduate majoring in English. At that time my response was to get angry at "The Darling" for lacking soul. The next time I read Chekhov was some years later, when I was preparing to teach several of his stories in an upper-division European literature course. By this time I had changed my tune a bit, so I presented *The Darling* to the class in a more sympathetic way. I tried to show the heroine as a victim of decadent, antifeminine society of turn-of-the-century Russia. Most of my students graciously responded by agreeing with me. Some of the more enlightened ones went so far as to

108

suggest that the story was "naturalistic," à la Thomas Hardy, and other sophisticates argued that it was "existential," with the heroine caught in the anxiety brought on by her discovery that the universe was an absurd void. Some of the slower students appeared to have no opinion on the story. It goes without saying that these students did poorly on the examination.

Several years after I taught that course, it occurred to me that my lecture and the class discussion of *The Darling* had left something out. We had neglected to consider whether it was valuable or important to have opinions in the first place. The Darling thought so, but did we? Chekhov apparently assumed it was important to have them, and my class and I had in effect shared his assumption without ever questioning it. We had never asked, "What's so sacred or precious about taking a stand?" My present answer is "Probably nothing." By that I mean that it is often less troublesome and more civilized to take no view at all. If more of us would go around without opinions, the world would probably not be so full of strife. It is of course necessary to have opinions on some things. My point is that we have them on too many things.

I think there is something in the basic nature of literature—and some of the other arts as well—that teaches the reader the idea that he absolutely must have many strong opinions. Literature does this in two ways: either it is opinionated or it is tantalizing unopinionated, so much so that we succumb to the urge to fill in the blanks and make doctrine and dogma out of the raw material furnished to us by the artist. There are numerous examples of both categories in English literature.

Opinionated writings, with the exception of the evasive ironies of Chaucer and of ballads like *The Two Ravens*, make up the bulk of Middle English literature. The doctrine of *Piers Plowman* is crystal clear and beautifully propounded to us in the discussion of "kind knowing" or natural knowledge that takes place between Holy Church and the Dreamer who narrates the poem. Other medieval English works in which the opinion is unequivocal are: *Sir Gawain and the Green Knight*, which grinds an axe about courtly responsibility and the dangers of excessive pride; *The Pearl*, with its emphasis on the medieval Christian attitude that *sic transit gloria mundi*; *Everyman*, which makes it clear that you can't take it with you; and *Morte D'arthur*, by Thomas Malory, who strongly upholds the chivalric and knightly ideals of such Arthurian predecessors as Geoffrey of Monmouth, Wace, Chrétien de Troyes, and Layamon.

If Middle English is by and large the domain of Opinion, the important writers of the next major period are marked by a coy refusal to take a stance. The great master here is, of course, Shakespeare, about whom it has been justly said that although he often probed the inner reaches of the psyche, he never revealed his own inner self. He is a master of ambivalence. One moment he is making Falstaff attractive, using him to satirize the Establishment, and the next moment he is portraying Sir John as a dirty old man who marches innocent starvelings off to the slaughter of the war, saying that they are "food for powder, food for powder; they'll fill a pit as well as better."

Shakespeare took no final stance, but in so beautifully refusing to take one, he has the opposite effect of strongly inviting us to take one. And we do. The vociferousness, the urgency, and the stubbornness of opinion about Shakespeare are enough to fill several shelves in any large university library. Volume upon volume of "distinguished" criticism reposes there in mute testimony to Shakespeare's ability to cause people to have opinions strong enough to write books about. The list of luminaries is huge, including the tightly argued theses of such heavyweights as A. C. Bradley, Caroline Spurgeon, John Dover Wilson, G. Wilson Knight, L. L. Schücking, and E. M. W. Tillyard. They all took their stand. The quickest way to offend an oldtime Shakespeare professor is to respond, when he calls on you, by saying you have no opinion on the play being discussed. There's a good chance that the professor will lose his temper, for to be without a view, a thesis, or a definite opinion is forbidden in the "discipline" of the "humanities."

The same attitude can be found among professors who teach the more modern, opinionated literature—"sociological" novelists like Upton Sinclair or Harvey Swados, or "school" poets like those in the "Fugitive" group. Opinionated writers turn us on or off. We tend either to be pulled in by their rhetoric or so offended by it that we violently disagree. Some of the most heated arguments I have witnessed among students of literature have centered on strongly opinionated writers like D. H. Lawrence. As students we were always told that it was "healthy" to argue about books, for it was the way to get rid of the bad ideas and ferret out the good ones. The truth, we were assured, was best arrived at through conflict, counterstatement, and dialectic. For this reason no student majoring in English is allowed to go through school without writing many term papers, in every one of which he is absolutely required to express his opinion.

The trend continues in graduate school, right through that ultimate tour de force of opinion which is so aptly named the thesis. It doesn't matter that there may already be an excess of opinion about literature; the paper-writing goes right on. Armed with his doctorate, the aspiring young professor begins to besiege the learned journals with articles. If his opinion is well argued, he will probably be published, adding to the already tumid store of opinion on the library shelves. For opinion is just about all that literary magazines print. Leafing through the pages of any number of *PMLA*'s *JEGP*'s, *MP*'s, or *PQ*'s will yield one hundred opinion-essays for every one that is purely factual. When the journals are not printing polemical articles, they are printing book reviews, which are by definition highly opinionated.

What is the first cause of this infinite mass of opinion that surrounds literature? The answer is literature itself. The nature of art begets opinion so consistently and compellingly that we simply cannot resist. Even vague or highly abstract art begets opinion. Few know what Ezra Pound is talking about in those later *Cantos*, but every reader has an opinion of them. A famous example in music occurred when Stravinski presented his *Rite of Spring* in Paris in 1913. It baffled the audience but at the same time caused so much fervent opinion that a riot broke out. The onslaught of opinion begotten by art is so overwhelming that we have trouble catching our breath long enough to ask why it is necessary to have an opinion in the first place.

We live in a civilization that believes that opinion per se is good. This can be seen in the very derivation of the word, which comes from the Latin *opinari*, meaning to think. It is a fundamental tenet of our civilization that thinking is good, a noble process which is one of the few things separating us from the base animal world. I too believe that thinking is a noble calling and that it is necessary to have opinions for the sake of the kind of thinking that can lead us to a better world.

In the world of the arts there is so much pressure on us to take a stand of some kind that all too often we are caught in a frantic, mindless search for something to say, anything. We become Darlings. Much of what appears in the learned journals and scholarly books is there because we have given in to the pressure to have a view of art or of a particular work of art. And the publishing is rewarded. The structure of the academic world is devised to stop those who have no opinion from getting ahead. I sometimes feel that it is these unopinionated persons who are the real heroes, though they are not only unsung but trampled on. Perhaps they should be rewarded for having the strength of character to avoid giving in to the seductions of art.

On the other hand, when I look at the scholarly articles and books I am struck by their almost universal phoniness. The thing that suggests to me that the author of a learned essay is a phony is not so much the particular opinion he has chosen as his eagerness to convince his audience that he has arrived at it through some laborious and careful thought process. In short, he doth protest too much. I suspect that if he had an honest and sincere opinion, there would be little need to preface it with fifteen or twenty pages of "argument" and "research."

Many of the most incisive and thoughtful opinions have been couched in brief, aphoristic terms: "Would God that all the Lord's people were prophets" (Numbers, XI.29). "Neither do men put new wine into old bottles" (Luke, IX.17). "Truth comes out in wine" (Pliny, *Historia Naturalis*, XIV.141). "It is human nature to despise the man you have hurt" (Tacitus, *Agricola*, 30). "To many, total abstinence is easier than perfect moderation" (St. Augustine, *On the Good of Marriage*, XXI). "The voice of the people is the voice of God" (Alcuin, *Letter to Charlemagne*). "Be a sinner and sin strongly, but more strongly have faith and rejoice in Christ" (Luther, *Letter to Melanchthon*). "Wear your learning like your watch, in a private pocket: and do not merely pull it out and strike it, merely to show that you have one" (Lord Chesterfield, *Letters to His Son*, March 9, 1748). "This was their finest hour" (Winston Churchill, Speech in the House of Commons, June 18, 1940). Each one of these is every inch an opinion. We can pull all of them out of context and they're still beautiful opinions. We can't do that with the snaggled sentences of the learned books and journals. This is not to deny that some good opinions have been very long. Most of them, however, are found outside of the world of art.

What should be done about the excess of unnecessary and sometimes dangerous opinion that surrounds the arts? Should it be suppressed or censored somehow? Should there be a moratorium on it? No, such measures would be impossible to enforce, and moreover there is already too much censorship in the world of art. Perhaps the best thing to do is simply to quit giving our students the impression that it's requisite or even chic to have an opinion on everything. We could do them a real service this way, for one of the great causes of narrowmindedness is the holding of strong opinions.

Section 2

The Misuse of Memory

I shall remember while the light lives yet
And in the night time I shall not forget.
　　　　　—Algernon Charles Swinburne, Erotion

In one of his letters to his son, Lord Chesterfield tried to quote a couplet from Pope: "A little learning is a dangerous thing;/ Drink deep or taste not the Castalian Spring." I say he "tried" to quote from Pope, because in fact the poet had written "Pierian Spring," not "Castalian." Chesterfield was widely—though superficially—read, and probably what threw him off was that he had too much general knowledge about Greek mythology. It's likely that he knew that the Nine Muses, who drank at the magic spring, are sometimes said to live on Mt. Pierus and sometimes on Mt. Parnassus. The sacred spring of knowledge on Mt. Pierus is the Pierian Spring, whereas on Mt. Parnassus it is called the Castalian Spring.

I have gone into this matter rather pedantically in order to illustrate the way that our memories play tricks on us when we are trying to recall works of art. There is a certain logic in the "fact" that the Muses, who are the inspirers of art, were all begotten by Zeus upon Mnemosyne or "Memory." For without strong remembrance of the past, there can be no art. It relies on the past, and it wouldn't be terribly inaccurate to call art, especially literature, a kind of frozen remembrance or suspended memory, to which we can always return with the comforting knowlege that here at least, here in the great painting or the memorable novel, we can find a piece of the past that hasn't changed. Solidified and preserved

113

exactly as we left it, the work of art is always there, ready for our return. At least a hundred times in my career, I have heard my teachers, colleagues, and students extoll this "virtue" of literature, its power to use the past to stabilize experience and thus impose order upon the vicissitudes of life.

It is certainly an irony, then, that the great books, those magical preservers of memory, are so hard to remember. Lord Chesterfield was by no means the first or last to have a literary memory that played tricks on him. Untotal recall is a common phenomenon among men of letters. One of the most touching moments in recent literary history occurred when Robert Frost was reciting to a large audience his "Stopping by Woods on a Snowy Evening." Frost was a very old man, and halfway through he forgot what came next. Another major American poet happened to be on the stage with him and whispered the next line, so that Frost was able to continue his recitation with minimum embarrassment.

When publicized, this gesture warmed the public's heart. But it also suggests once again, Frost's senility notwithstanding, that there is something in the nature of literature that can make it hard to remember. When Frost forgot his own line, his mind went blank so that he remembered nothing in its stead. He did not make the Chesterfieldian mistake of supplying something of his own in place of the original. There are, then, two basic methods of forgetting literature. One is to blank it out (Frostian) and the other is to displace and supplant it (Chesterfieldian).

We should acknowledge here that of course anything under the sun is potentially forgettable. It is just that art, literature especially, seems so well-suited to be forgotten. Anyone who has taught a large literature survey course will know what I mean. In looking over hundreds of flounderings and booboos committed on student examinations, I have frequently observed that the Chesterfieldian-replacement kind of forgetting occurs much more often than the Frostian blank. The majority, rather than admit defeat, will make a desperate attempt to recall the image, line, or passage. I used to think this happened because of the pressure of the exams, but later I got to noticing that many non-students—writers, professors, general readers—had the same habit. I saw that at literary cocktail parties it seemed socially acceptable to misquote or misstate a literary work; but forgetting it altogether was strictly taboo. I came to realize the magnitude of the disaster that would have occurred if someone had not come to Frost's rescue.

What is it about art that makes it so eminently forgettable? I think it has to do with what might be called "excess of memory." We see such an excess in elderly people, whom we often characterize as having weak memories, a sure sign, so we like to think, of senility. I remember being shocked when an elderly aunt of mine, whom I hadn't seen for several years, called me by someone else's name. She thought I was my cousin. A short time later she made another "mistake" by thinking I was her son-in-law. Later that day she finally got me "right." Poor woman, I thought, to be so confused.

It occurred to me later that her "confusion" was the kind that only a person of great knowledge and experience could be capable of. The memory of an aged person is like a palimpsest, a piece of parchment that has been written on many times and imperfectly erased, so that one can still read many of the words from long ago. The trouble with the elderly aunt was not that she remembered too little but rather that she remembered too much. When she saw me, she could think of a number of possibilities as to my identity. It would be hard for a younger, less-experienced person to make such a mistake.

The excess of memory that troubled the old woman is not unlike a literary person's memory. He is heavily stocked with not only his own experience but also that of many authors and the dozens of persons those authors have written about. I think it is possible to have ingested so much vicarious life from novels, poems, and plays that one finally reaches the point where he cannot, even if he tries, completely separate truth from fiction. It embarrasses me that sometimes I have caught myself thinking that I have done or said something, when in fact I haven't.

I have had too much experience. A hundred times at least, I have lived through the labors, ordeals, triumphs or joys of youth, maturity and old age. Born and killed a hundred times, I have been the distraught lover, the epic warrior, the scapegoat, the traitor, the innocent lamb, the martyr, the tyrannical father, the Prodigal Son, the Wandering Jew, the Wounded King, and a hundred other creatures of suffering or triumph. I was with Pandora when she opened the box, and I will have a ringside seat at Armageddon. It was not until Walt Whitman had read for years that he could say (in *Song of Myself*), "I am large, I contain multitudes." Virtually anyone in the "humanities" will tell you that this is a good way to be.

Not necessarily. One trouble with containing multitudes is that it can deprive us of ourselves. We are so busy being someone else—Oedipus, Gargantua, Huckleberry Finn, Augie March—that we don't have time to be what we originally were. A more serious trouble with the world of fiction is that it not only distorts our memories but makes us comfortable in the distortion. The language of art is such that its sweet music and subtle rhetoric cajole us into relaxing and acquiescing in the luxury of memories that don't belong to us. The two lines preceding Whitman's "I am large, I contain multitudes" are: "Do I contradict myself?/ Very well, then I contradict myself." The tone of these words is a gleeful contempt, a nonchalant eschewing of literal truth.

I think that what Whitman says is what many literary people do. They have lived so long in a misty halfworld comprised of fact and fiction that they have gotten comfortably used to confusing one with the other. They have made a successful adjustment to telling lies and not being bothered at all about having done so. There was a time when I was appalled at the great number of prevaricators and distortionists in the "humanities." I was amazed at what I thought was a contrast between the veracities of art and the palpable falsehoods of my colleagues and, too frequently, myself. More lately I have come to believe that no such contrast exists. Considered as a whole, literature, with its excess of memory, furnishes the seeds of dishonesty that we nurture in ourselves as students and teachers and scholars.

I haven't meant to imply that people making their careers in literature go around like blatant Pinocchios, telling whoppers. Liars in the literary world are more subtle, as the following example should illustrate. Several years ago a young man I'd known and liked in graduate school applied for an assistant professorship at the college where I was teaching. We were interested enough in him to send for his "credentials"—a confidential file containing letters of recommendation which the candidate is not allowed to see. The letters in my friend's file were highly favorable, except for one. Surprisingly, it was written by a professor who had given him an "A" and had praised his work many times. I was surprised to see that the same professor in the confidential letter referred to my friend as "immature," "irascible," and "too aggressive." I immediately wrote to my friend to tell him about what had been written of him. He was as amazed as I had been. In the meantime, the letter had done its damage. Our college decided not to hire him, even though I had tried to defend him by pointing to the contradictory origin of the letter. Sorry, said our dean and our chairman: we have got to be completely sure about him, and one bad letter can't be ignored.

I didn't know what if anything my friend did to deserve an unfavorable letter in his credentials. All I knew was that he who wrote it was a dishonest man who smiled in your face and stabbed you in the back. I got to wondering what would make a person do a thing like that. Then I began to recall that in my career I had seen dozens of people in the "humanities" do things like that. And I wondered if it could be merely an accident that so many cheaters and liars are to be found in the "profession" of teaching the arts on the college level. I don't think so. I think that the powerful fictions of literature and the other arts, furnishing us with an excess of identities, make us relax in the big lie, so that we can behave as the smiling letter writing professor did and lose no sleep over it.

In his essay, *On Liars,* Montaigne divides the tellers of falsehoods into two categories: those who intentionally lie and those who are merely misinformed. Then he goes on to describe a habitual liar he knows: "I have an honest lad to my tailor, whom I never knew guilty of one truth, no, not even when it was to his advantage. If falsehood had, like truth, only one face, we would be upon better terms. For we would then take for truth the opposite of what the liar says. But the reverse of truth has a hundred thousand forms, and a field indefinite, without bound or limit." My view is that too many of us in the "humanities" are habitual liars. We have a very real psychological need to falsify things. Steeped in the hundred thousand forms of fiction, we too often find ourselves morally adrift.

Section 3

The
Misuse
of
Evidence

Be sure of it; give me the ocular proof.

—Othello, *III. iii.*

There are any number of ways we can read the fourth Book of *Gulliver's Travels,* in which Gulliver meets the Houyhnhnms, those highly intelligent horses who seem to be the embodiment of pure reason.

One interpretation of this troublesome section of Swift's classic is that the author thinks man is condemned to be no better than the disgusting Yahoos, creatures who look like men but behave in a bestial manner. Another interpretation is that Swift, who once described man as *rationis capax*—"capable of reason"—wants us to use our rational faculties to become like the Houyhnhnms. Still another view is that the Book posits a golden mean (in the character of Don Pedro, the gentle Portuguese captain) between the overheated passions of the Yahoos and the cold, austere reason of the horses. It has also been argued that Swift is a kind of early existentialist who wishes us to strive for the unattainable ideal of reason even though we can't reach it, because there is dignity in the striving itself, as Camus said of Sisyphus rolling his stone. Then there is the thesis that Swift takes no position at all because he is merely writing a comedy.

There are other readings too, but the ones I've mentioned should be enough to suggest that Book Four of *Gulliver's Travels* is wide open for interpretation. Scholars have argued about it for years, and the end is nowhere in sight. Moreover, most of the arguments are conducted in a sound scholarly manner, logically argued and solidly documented. We would not have to feel embarrassed if we caught ourselves agreeing heartily with all of them.

What happens in *Gulliver's Travels* is what happens with a great many classics in literature. Scholars are irresistibly drawn toward them, and interpretations proliferate. Some other masterpieces in English which are surrounded by scads of interpretation are the anonymous medieval *Pearl*, a number of Chaucer's *Canterbury Tales*, *Hamlet* of course, *Paradise Lost*, much of Blake, most of Eliot, and all of Joyce. We simply cannot get near these writings without having to flounder through a morass of scholarship and criticism. Even the less famous works of English literature carry with them sizeable accretions of "learning," so that wherever we go, we are liable to encounter the Cerberus of pedantry, who barks us away from the things we might like to read. If we listen closely, we realize that this mythological creature is saying: Keep out! Members only! This book is not for general dissemination!

I am reminded of Eleanor Prescott Hammond, the eminent old-time bibliographer of Chaucer studies. The three-headed preface to her *Chaucer: A Bibliographical Manual* is a warning, not an invitation:

> Suggestions or sketches for a bibliography of Chaucer have been made by J. E. B. Mayor in Notes and Queries 1876 II: 530; by J. Maskell in the same journal 1883 II: 381, 1844 I: 138, 141, 361, 422, 462, II: 3, 64, 422; in the Boston Literary World 14: 288 (1883); by Henry B. Wheatley before the Bibliographical Society in March, 1884, see their Transactions vol. II, pp. 11-12. The reference lists in Sonnenschein's Best Books and in Koerting's Grundriss zur Geschichte der englischen Literatur, 2d ed. Munster 1893, are avowedly brief and partial; and Courtney's Register of National Bibliography, 1905, has under Chaucer but five entries. The Chaucer-bibliography appended to Vol. II of the Cambridge History of English Literature, which appears just as this volume goes to press, is of necessity condensed; but its choice of entries is irregular and uncritical, and it is defaced by numerous misstatements; e.g., it lists editions of "Chaucer's Works" by Sir Harris Nicolas and by Tyrwhitt.

She goes on to say that her manual does not

> attempt to record all the lighter "literary" essays contained in the files of periodicals appealing to the younger or the very general reader; again, the section upon the life of Chaucer does not comprise such third-hand biographies as are usually printed in school manuals of literature, but deals with those accounts of Chaucer based upon direct investigation, or

presumably so based, with notes upon early biographies which age has now rendered curiosities of criticism.

Who does she think she's talking to? She makes us think of signs we have seen on barbed-wire fences surrounding military bases.

Yet there is a problem with Chaucer too, for without him there could be no Eleanor Prescott Hammonds. The fact that great art is so often surrounded by polemical scholarship and criticism moves us to the conclusion that there is something in the basic nature of art that causes people to argue about it. At one time I thought that the argument-causing property of art was simply its emotional content and sense of excitement. It gets us all stirred up, causing us to make strong statements about it, which are apt to be refuted or argued with by others who have also been stirred up.

More recently, I have come to believe that in addition to the excitement of art there is another argument-causing ingredient, which might be called excess of evidence. I am referring to the way that art so fiercely concentrates on whatever it has chosen for its topic, marshalling innumerable "facts" about it, until the audience is all but satiated with "knowledge" of the subject. In painting, we see an excess of evidence in the way the artist interprets the human face so that we "see" more of it than if it were merely photographed, as in Rembrandt's penetrating self-portrait of himself in old age, or as in some of Picasso's cubistic works, in which we see a person's head from several angles at the same time.

The same sort of excess seems to occur in classical music and in progressive jazz, in which we hear a number of explorations of, or variations on, the same theme. For example, the famous jazz saxophonist Stan Getz characteristically begins by playing two or three successive, different improvisations on the same melody, after which he breaks into even freer improvisations which depart altogether from the original melody, retaining only a loose allegiance to the harmony or basic chord structure. Yet at the end of a Getz performance, we have the definite impression that he stayed always on the same subject, thoroughly teaching it to us, describing it in infinite detail, so that we have the feeling of excessive knowledge about it.

Such a feeling isn't much different from that which a great book gives us. After finishing *Madame Bovary*, even the least sensitive readers would have the impression that Flaubert's intense "study" of her had laid her character bare, furnishing the audience with nothing less than encyclopedic knowledge of her decrepit soul. Understandably, one comes away with the conviction that he is an absolute expert on Madame Bovary. I have heard several literary people say that one earmark of a great book is that it succeeds in giving the reader the impression that he knows more about the book's topic than anyone else in the world, including the author! Such is the power of great art. It gives us the illusion that there is a special, intimate relationship between ourselves and the artist's subject, and sometimes we have the feeling that no one else even knows that the subject exists.

When I am reading *Hamlet* I often develop an urge to *tell* people about it, as if the Melancholy Dane's history had heretofore been classified as a top secret. I am bursting with information about Hamlet, so filled am I by the massive "evidence" presented by Shakespeare. So I sit down at my writing table and begin to put together an essay or a lecture in which I seem to extract a thesis out of the evidence in the play. I say "seem" because I think I actually begin with some kind of preconceived idea which rather automatically causes me to arrange the play's evidence to accommodate my thesis. If I am guilty of such a priori thinking, I attribute it to the excessive evidence in the writings of Shakespeare and many other major authors. They give me so much that I can find nearly anything I want. If I wish Hamlet to be an Oedipal figure, I can prove "conclusively" that he is. I shall have equal success if I attempt to prove that he is a stock Senecan revenge character, a typical example of Renaissance melancholy, an Aristotelian tragic hero, an existentialist, or a scholastic, or all of these rolled together. I can't lose; the evidence for all of my theses is overwhelmingly present in the rich and abundant language of the play. Shakespeare has given me a deck of cards, which I can shuffle, cut, and arrange in a nearly infinite number of ways.

Great literature is rich and many sided, always presenting us with an excess of evidence. We like it that way too. One of the nicest things we can say about a work of art is that it's complex; and woe unto the artist whose work the critics have branded as "simple," "transparent," or "one dimensional." A sure way to fail as a creative writer is to offer the reader the kind of evidence that can be used or interpreted in only one unequivocal way. Such is the fate of many novels, plays and poems in which the political, sociological, or philosophical content is too manifest, too clear.

American literature seems to have more than its share of authors who ground their axes with too noisy a rasp. We read their works as historical documents, museum pieces, or potboilers rather than as works of art. I am thinking of such minor figures as a Royal Tyler, John Trumbull, William Gilmore Simms, Charles Dudley Warner, Robert Herrick, Edward Bellamy, and Ayn Rand. They were all learned, sophisticated, and articulate, but they failed to give us that excess of evidence that we crave. So we return to our Henry Jameses, our Sherwood Andersons, our William Faulkners. For only here, in the deeper brakes and thickets of art, can we experience that mystical union of bewilderment and syntax which constitutes literary thinking. A central difficulty with great art is that in order to be great it has to be able to cause us, through its excess of evidence, to think unclearly about it.

One would think that our constant exposure to the massive evidence of literature would eventually have the effect of making us experts in handling and interpreting evidence. Theoretically, the more we do something, the better we should be at doing it. But it doesn't seem to work that way. Literary study more often seems to have the effect of making people profoundly casual if not downright irresponsible in the use of evidence—and in the use of those near-relations of evidence, reason and logic. Uncannily, those who live with the great books often display the ability to wrestle expertly with literary evidence all day and then, when they turn to political or other practical matters, they can suddenly behave as if they never heard of evidence.

I remember two bright, eloquent young professors in an English department at a major university who decided one day that the existing English major program ought to be immediately junked and replaced with a different program of their own invention. The fundamental difference between the old and the proposed new major was that the old was a chronological approach (Old English, Middle English, Renaissance, Seventeenth Century, etc.) and the new was an approach according to genres, traditions, or modes (tragedy, comedy, lyric, romance, etc.). When a senior member of the department asked one of the proponents to define "genre" or "mode" more closely, he was unable to do so. He seemed somewhat miffed at the question. He said everybody already knew fairly well what a genre was. When he was questioned further, he mentioned several literary theorists (Wellek, Austin Warren, Frye, Holland, and Hough), but still didn't make himself clear.

The amazing thing was that the new program, full of vagaries and enigmas as it was, was voted through and adopted! I think it was due to the slick salespitch given to the department. It certainly couldn't have had anything to do with evidence for anything. And at no time during the discussion were the crucial questions asked: What kind of results, if any, is the present program getting? What kind of results are desirable? What assurance is there that the new program will get the right results?

I think that the reason these questions weren't asked is that they would have thrust the department members into an embarrassing confrontation with the very thing they wanted to avoid: a sustained immersion in hard thinking based on hard evidence of the kind which could have been obtained through surveys or other studies of persons in English before, during and after college. But that would have been too much bother, would have taken too much time, would have been too rigorous, or (to use what is a dirty word in the "humanities") would have been too much like what they did in the *social sciences*. Hardly anyone, incidentally, hates statistics as much as English teachers do.

How did it come about, this hiatus between the excessive evidence of literature and the off-the-top-of-the-head generalizations we start making as soon as we shut our books and step into the faculty meeting? A possible answer is that we are struggling to avoid a busman's holiday. Steeped in evidence most of our working day, we don't want any more to do with it once we have stopped our reading, writing, and teaching.

Thus the department meeting emerges as a kind of recess, a free, exciting time when we can loosen up and shoot the bull with colleagues we haven't seen all week. Maybe we can blow off a little steam and get rid of some hostilities too. All of us who have sojourned in literary Academe are acquainted with that pleasant sensation of excitement that hits us as we walk into the meeting room. And deep inside, we may feel that we can forgive ourselves if during the meeting we make some pretty extravagant statements and do some pretty extravagant things. The lid's off, and we're in no hurry to put it back on. Such is the corrupting influence of the great books.

Section 4

The
Misuse
of
Ideas

Delightful task! to rear the tender thought,
To teach the young idea how to shoot.
—*James Thomson,* The Seasons *(Spring)*

In my second year of college I had a real dynamo of an English professor for an introduction to literature course. He was young, maybe thirty-one or two, and he had done his Ph.D. dissertation, he told us, on Theodore Dreiser. He cheerfully admitted that in the course of writing his thesis he had gotten completely hooked on Naturalism, especially on the fatalistic aspects of it. After reading masses of Stephen Crane, Frank Norris, Hamlin Garland, and Dreiser, he had become a full-scale determinist.

Many times we listened with genuinely rapt attention while the enthusiastic professor explained to us that the sole reason we were sitting in his class was that certain biological and sociological forces had put us there. Free choice had nothing to do with it. We were shocked and delighted upon learning this strange fact about ourselves. We were not free! The sudden acquiring of this knowledge was like being sprung from a dark prison of ignorance and getting a lungful of intellectual fresh air. And so we went the way most sophomores majoring in English go. We became full-scale, militant, atheistical determinists. We were grateful to our teacher for showing us the way.

My schedule was such that I didn't have another course from him until the next academic year. I found him a changed man. Not that he had lost any of his fire—he still had that, all right—but his philosophy seemed completely opposite from what it had been a year earlier. Now, instead of Naturalistic determinism, he wholeheartedly embraced Sartrean Existentialism and fervently preached its virtues. The course I now had from him was modern drama, which is commonly known to be rife with existential attitudes, so I thought that he might be changing his tune to fit the subject matter he was now teaching. Even so, it seemed rather shallow to me, doing a philosophical about-face as glibly and as effortlessly as he seemed to have done it. What had become of his passionate determinism of only one year ago? How could he discard it so easily? I was troubled because Naturalism and Existentialism seemed to be exact opposites. I wouldn't have been bothered if he had merely shifted from, say, the idealism of Kant to that of Fichte, for these two are comfortable bedfellows, and the latter may be looked upon as little more than an extension of the former.

But Naturalism and Existentialism! These were 180 degrees from each other! On the one side stood the great Naturalistic novelists like the Goncourts, Zola, Hardy, Crane, and Drieser, chanting practically in unison that man is so unfree that it's frightening. On the other side were the Existentialists like Unamuno, Sartre, Camus, Beckett, and Colin Wilson, chanting right back that, on the contrary, man is so free that it's frightening—"dreadful freedom," to use the fashionable phrase.

As soon as I had a chance, I waylaid the professor after class and politely demanded to know what had caused him to go so quickly from one philosophy to the other. He seemed eager to answer me, though not in philosophical terms. Rather than refuting the doctrine of Naturalism or defending that of the Existentialists, he began to talk about the "necessity and the duty" of keeping one's flexibility and detachment in the world of ideas. It was important, he said, to avoid being taken completely in by any doctrine or set of values, no matter how beautifully convincing it might seem. He paraphrased T. S. Eliot's famous pronouncement that Henry James had a mind so fine that no idea could violate it. What Eliot meant was that James could regularly use powerful ideas in his art without being brainwashed or corrupted by them. Then he quoted the advice that James gives at the end of his well-known essay, *The Art of Fiction:* "Do not think too much about optimism and pessimism; try to catch the color of life itself." That's the way we should all be, the professor said, totally involved in life but always keeping the various doctrines and philosophies at arm's length.

At this point I excused myself and went down the hall and out the door to get some fresh air. Even an ingenue like myself could see that this teacher was a phony, that he didn't care about ideas any more than the man in the moon, that he put them on or off as if they were badges or hats, excusing his intellectual fickleness with a verbal smokescreen about detachment and flexibility and all that.

What I failed to see until many years later was that he was only a slight exaggeration of most English professors, for it took an embarrassingly long time for me to get it through my head that one of the many ways that literature corrupts those who study it is its inherent casualness about ideas. Suddenly, after God knows how many semesters of teaching English at the college level, I came to see that art by its very definition *had* to be irresponsible with ideas, doctrines, values, or ideals.

To see the truth of this proposition, one had only to consider its opposite. Take for example rigid sociological novels like Sinclair's *The Jungle*, or excessively doctrinal poems like Joel Barlow's *Columbiad*. One didn't have to immerse himself in second rate art like this very long to come to the following conclusion: The more openly committed the artist is to his ideas, the less seriously we take his art. On the other hand, the great works always seemed to have about them a beautiful detachment and distance from doctrines, philosophies, or solidified attitudes of any kind. Look at Shakespeare: nobody could ever pin him down ideologically; he seemed at once to believe in everything and nothing.

Even when literary history could place a writer precisely within a tradition, that writer was looked upon as a good writer only insofar as he could keep himself free .of the manifestos or values of the school or tradition to which he belonged. Thus although Thomas Gray was the best of the "Graveyard Poets," he was great partly by means of maintaining a skepticism toward certain graveyard-poetry ideals, one of them being the ideal of a kind of Rousseauean solitude and isolation; for Gray in his *Elegy Written in a Country Churchyard* is eminently societal, peopling his thoughts with images of busy villages and "madding crowds," even though the ostensible direction of his meaning is toward the narrow oneness of the grave. This famous poem, which forever seems to promise an ideal and a value of loneliness, delivers instead a busy pluralism and a philosophy committed to life on this earth. The final effect is one of ambivalence. If we turn to a Graveyard Poet who is excessively committed to the ideas and attitudes of his school, we end up not taking him seriously at all. Every time I teach Robert Blair's *The Grave*, the students laugh at it. They simply can't groove on a serious level with those tombs that are described as "Furred round with mouldy damps and ropy slime."

For some reason, the later eighteenth century in England is full of writers whose art suffers from this excessive commitment to the doctrines of their traditions. Henry Mackenzie, who wrote *The Man of Feeling*, surely could have reduced the level of silliness in this light novel if he had believed less fervently in the philosophy of Sensibility. Ann Radcliffe would be taken more seriously as a novelist if she had taken Gothicism less seriously. Elizabeth Inchbald, in her too honest dichotomy of the "natural" and the "civilized," has ensured her novel called *Nature and Art* a place among the less-important English novels. Similarly, William Godwin's *Caleb Williams*, a novel about the bullying powers of the upper classes, is so clear-cut in its message that it is almost always excluded from courses in the novel.

In offering many examples of writers who ruined themselves artistically by being too committed to doctrine, the eighteenth century differs from other literary periods only in degree, not in kind. Any era will yield many "failures" of this sort. If we are unaware of the extent to which so many writers fail through excessive commitment, it is only because our English classes concentrate rather exclusively on the ones who write with a beautiful ironic detachment, who tease and tantalize rather than teach us, forever dangling the hints of ideas or attitudes just above or below us where we can't quite reach them.

I remember how it was when I was working for my degrees. The major writers were always intellectually elusive; I never knew exactly where they stood, philosophically speaking. Neither did the major critics. I could read volumes of high-powered criticism on every big writer from Shakespeare to Shaw, from Fielding to Forster, from the Middle English Lyric to Wallace Stevens, and after I got through I knew what I knew before I started—that they were geniuses—but I still had only a faint or foggy comprehension of their actual philosophies, doctrines, or ideals.

And that was all we were supposed to have. When I was in school it was constantly preached in the classroom that the beauty and value of the great books was their intellectual detachment. Any novel, play, or poem that took too definite a stand was a bad one, we were told. The function of a classic seemed to be to convince its readers that it was loaded with ideas and at the same time keep these ideas partially veiled in layers of complex imagery or narrative. We ended up with the frustrating feeling of knowing they were there but not being able to get to them.

After a while this almost-but-not-quite trick of the major authors began to soften our brains. Without realizing what had happened to us, we began to behave as though ideas didn't count, as though they had no consequences. Subconsciously we had come to the conclusion that because the great books were distant and irresponsible in the use of ideas, it was all right for us to be that way too. That was what had happened in the back of the brain of the professor who had gone from Naturalistic determinism to Existentialism as easily as jumping across a mud puddle. That was what happened in the minds of all of us who published books or articles in which we so seriously argued such-and-such a thesis, only to do an about-face a few years later and argue its precise antithesis.

Such a switch is often "explained" or "justified" on the grounds that we have matured in our thinking or that we are broadminded and flexible enough to admit that we were a bit wrong in our previous publications. Such elasticity, we like to think, is squarely within the great tradition of humanism. Indeed, it's fashionable to keep changing our scholarly ideas, and the professor who hammers the same thesis for twenty years becomes a laughingstock among his colleagues—Oh, is he still on that old hobby horse? The thing to do is to stay alive, keep "growing," as I must admit I have done all through my career, though at this late stage I'm not sure what I've grown into.

Whatever it is, I'm not sure I like it. At one time or the other I have been Platonist, Aristotelian, Augustinian, Renaissance Humanist, Hobbist, Berkeleyan, Kantian, Darwinian, Sartrean, and you-name-it. I can't say it has been good for me. If anything, it has driven me perilously close to the idea that ideas don't have any consequences, an attitude from which I am just now in my middle age beginning to try to escape.

I want to embrace the attitude that if excessive commitment is bad, commitment to nothing, as in the greatest art, is even worse. I want somehow to be on guard against the sly way in which great literature has the capacity to make us think it propounds ideas when it doesn't. In a crazy way the great books have the power to get us into a fanatical excitement about ideas and at the same time make us disdainful of the seriousness and consequences of ideas.

I'm not sure just what it is in literature that causes those who study it to get simultaneously excited and overcasual about ideas. Possibly the trouble stems from the typical English professor's daily overexposure to comparisons, analogies, or metaphors. It's worth looking at these standard literary devices for a moment. In Part I, Chapter 8, of *The*

Leviathan, Hobbes referred to the comparison-making faculty of mind as "fancy" and made a distinction between "fancy" and "judgment":

> And whereas in this succession of men's thoughts, there is nothing to observe in the things they think on, but either in what they be like one another, or in what they be unlike . . .; those that observe their similtudes, in case they be such as are but rarely observed by others, are said to have a good wit; by which, in this occasion, is meant a good fancy. But they that observe their differences and dissimiltudes, which is called distinguishing and discerning and judging between thing and thing, in case such discerning be not easy, are said to have a good judgment.

Hobbes may have found the germ of the idea in Bacon's *Novum Organum,* which tells us that "some are more vigorous and active in observing the differences of things, other in observing their resemblances" (Bl.I; Aph. 55). In any case, a moment's reflection should bring us to the observation that without the ability to make clever comparisons, that is without "fancy," no creative writer could get very far. Without fancy there would be no metaphorical language, and the great books would have to get along without such celebrated figurative breakthroughs as Homer's "wine-dark sea," Donne's comparison of lovers and compasses in his *Valediction Forbidding Mourning,* or Eliot's description in *Prufrock* of the evening as "spread out against the sky/ Like a patient etherized upon a table." Also missing would be such superb images as "take arms against a sea of troubles," "my love is like a red red rose," "nature red in tooth and claw," and thousands of other fine symbols and figures of speech, without which the great books would cease to be literature. Milton, who professed in his *Paradise Lost* to "liken spiritual to corporeal form," could never have written his epic, nor could any other epic have been written. There would be no *Faerie Queene, Arcadia, Orlando Furioso, Jerusalem Delivered, Morte D'arthur, Divine Comedy, Thebaid,* or *Aeneid.*

For the mainspring of nearly all that's powerful or fascinating in literature is the artist's uncanny ability to find similarities between things apparently unlike. Those comparable but dissimilar things may be small, like the fistlike face on the corpse in Dylan Thomas' *In Memory of Anne Jones;* or they may be large, whole modes of existence, as in Joyce's *Ulysses,* which is a sustained analogy for the world of Homer's *Odyssey.* The only rule seems to be that they be simultaneously alike and unlike. Twentieth-century critics tend to feel that the more farfetched the comparison is, the better it is, which accounts for the revival of interest in

Donne and the Metaphysical School of poetry, and for the disinterment of such long forgotten metaphorical extravagancies as Joshua Sylvester's description of snowflakes that "periwig with snow the bald-pate woods."

Now, we know that snow is not a wig and that the woods don't have a bald head. However, we are usually willing to indulge the poet while he makes his metaphorical point. And we love the excitement we feel when the writer discerns a striking new similarity between two things that we thought had nothing to do with each other. Who would have thought that fame was "like a wayward girl," until John Keats came along? But after we have read a great deal, we can begin to acquire the habit and the skill of seeing resemblances for ourselves, without having others point them out for us. It is a delicious and exciting experience, this play of "fancy" (to use Hobbes' term). At this point we may graduate to the status of literary critics who have the ability to make ingenious comparisons among different authors or works, or between a particular work and an idea, as happens in a Marxist interpretation of the *Faerie Queene,* an Oedipal analysis of *Hamlet,* or a Christian-allegorical reading of *The Red Badge of Courage.*

The interpretative business of literary criticism and teaching literature is by and large the business of making clever comparisons, and as such it provides a strong stimulus to our native fancy. Over the years it sharpens our imaginative eyesight so that we can find similarities between practically any pair of ideas or things one can name. In the mind of the seasoned English professor, everything is potentially everything else. It's my opinion that once a person has reached this mental state, he begins to lose whatever set of values he might have started out with. Because everything is so similar to him, everything may eventually seem to take on the same value or importance as everything else. To him, one idea commences to be as good as any other idea, making it easy now to go quickly from one philosophy to another, with relative comfort and virtually no sense of intellectual upheaval. He is a philosophical vagrant now, overcasual about ideas and their consequences, but he doesn't become blasé or bored. On the contrary, his perpetual exposure to the dynamite of the great books, together with the thrills of the comparisons he himself makes, keeps him eager and enthusiastic about ideas, even while in actual practice he doesn't give a damn about them.

I think this helps to explain the professor who slid so easily from Naturalistic determinism to Existentialism. I can remember him at one time actually trying to lecture on some "similarities" between the two philosophies, and I recall coming away totally unconvinced, with the feeling that he was blurring distinctions right and left. This was before I knew anything about Hobbes or "fancy," so I could not have seen at that time that the professor, like too many people in the "humanities," was suffering from an excess of "fancy" and a lack of "judgment," which in Hobbes' words is "distinguishing and discerning and judging between thing and thing." I could not have seen at that time that literature has the power to make liars out of us without our even knowing it. Nor could I have seen that it can muddle our thinking and subtly escort us to the point where we can't even communicate because we are on too many wavelengths at the same time.

If playing with ideas were a harmless sport (I've heard one professor describe it as "good intellectual exercise"), there would be nothing to worry about. The trouble is, ideas do have consequences, as even the cheapest demagogue will tell us. From Jericho to Buchenwald, most of the atrocities in history can be traced to some tribe or tyrant getting hooked on an idea and using it in an irrational and dangerous way.

The insidious thing about ideas is that we can't see their effects right away; it takes a while for them to do the good or the damage that they're capable of. It's not like surgery or auto mechanics where you see your results in a fairly short time. The delayed reaction of ideas theoretically should make us all the more cautious in handling them. But it seems to have the opposite effect. Because we can't see any results right away, we tend not to care as much as we should. And if literature has made us casual and unserious about ideas in the first place, we have the potential of becoming a real menace. Teaching English, which is inevitably to teach ideas, can be a heavy responsibility. However, the very nature of ideas and of the way they're handled in the great books tends to make us irresponsible.

Part V

Four Ways of Failing to Communicate

Section 1

Why We Distort the Language

And torture one poor word ten thousand ways.
          —*John Dryden*, Mac Flecknoe

A friend of mine is a whiz at making puns. His greatest tour de force occurred some years ago in San Francisco, in the heyday of the topless dancer. He and I had gone to an overpriced nightclub to watch the famous Carole Doda cavort around, and after the show I asked him what he thought of Miss Doda's act. "Well," he shrugged, "if you've seen two, you've seen 'em all." This fine pun later appeared in *Time* magazine (a storehouse of wordplay), but it was original with my friend. When he saw that I enjoyed his "seen 'em all" joke, he went on to make further puns. He said that Miss Doda needed more support from the band. That she appeared to have been drinking, though she wasn't in her cups. That she might end up in the booby hatch.

My friend is a salesman, a successful one, though he majored in English in college. After he graduated (Phi Beta Kappa), he started to work toward his master's degree, but after only one term he quit and went into the business world, never to return. When asked about his reasons for quitting graduate school, he smiles and says he got tired of being poor. I suspect, however, that he had become generally disillusioned with the "humanities." He often makes jaundiced remarks about what he sees as the disparity between the supposed high ideals of art and the morally sleazy behavior of the people who create it, study it, and teach it. He likes to hold forth on his favorite thesis that although business people may be no better than art people, they are certainly no worse.

He is a Republican, though not a vociferous one. He doesn't like campaign slogans or political propaganda. Once, when we were having an argument, I tried to make the point that, like any salesman, he used slogans and propaganda in his selling. He said that serious salespeople didn't use as much of this as English teachers thought they did. I thought then of how many times in lectures I'd used businessmen as scapegoats without knowing anything about business—hadn't I used slogans and propaganda here? Sensing that he had backed me into a corner, my friend pressed his attack. He said that because no creative writer used language in a responsible way, it could be assumed that those who taught literature would be irresponsible in their language too. He said this as a kind of joke, but I think I detected a hard edge of conviction under his humor.

After that argument, I got to thinking about the possible connections between my friend's distrust of the "humanities" and his pun making (which has been less persistent since he left graduate school). I came up with the theory that his punning might have been his way of using up the excess linguistic energies which he had acquired during his years of literary study. Reading too many heavy books seems to have the effect of opening up a plethora of possibilities for the use of language and of making us too good at words—though not necessarily good in our sentence structure or general writing style. What do you do when you're good at something but have no serious way to use your skill? My friend's solution was to make puns. It's worth examining this brand of humor for a moment.

What happens when a person makes a pun? For one thing, his audience may groan. But what happens in the psyche and in the mechanics of language? A basic ingredient of virtually any kind of comedy or humor is incongruity. What usually happens when we make a joke is that we bring together two areas of thought, imagery, or action that may have some remote resemblance to each other but are seldom found together. This is what happens in all puns. When my friend said that Carole Doda might end up in the booby hatch, he produced an incongruous relationship between breasts and insane asylums. A punster loves to fracture or destroy the established order of things. He has a keen sense of the potential absurdity of a universe in which drinking glasses can be turned into brassieres.

The ability to perceive such incongruities is a talent that people have called by many names. In the seventeenth century it was known as "wit" and was sometimes looked upon as a trivial or even destructive habit of mind. In his famous essay, "Laughter," Henri Bergson invented the elaborate term "reciprocal interference of series" to describe puns and several other sorts of comic incongruities. Like the older critics (e.g., Hobbes, Locke, and Addison) and like his contemporary Freud, Bergson sees comedy and humor as potentially hostile. He wrote that in order for us to laugh at something, we have to undergo a "temporary anesthetizing of the heart" and that the comic always seems to be predicated on "an unavowed intention to humiliate."

However that may be, there does appear to be a price tag on the comic; somebody always has to be the butt of the humor. In a drama, narrative, or joke, it may be a scapegoat or fool within the fiction, but in a pun it often seems to be the listener himself. He has been suckered into believing that the punster is making a serious point until it is suddenly revealed that he had no intention of being serious. If a series of puns ceases to be funny, as is often the case, that is because the element of surprise (another basic ingredient of humor) is gone. I think that people who are bad or tedious punsters may be subconsciously seeking to humiliate themselves and that good punsters like my friend may subconsciously seek to belittle their audiences.

I haven't meant to imply that my friend is any more hostile than the average person. If he has belittled me with wordplay, he has done it in a gentle and fun loving manner. As I said earlier, there is a price tag on the comic, but my friend offers it to everyone at a generous discount. Perhaps he is a bit of an exception. Over the years, I have noticed that those who pun a great deal are often highly excitable persons with more than the usual share of hostility. An outstanding example is James Joyce, especially as he shows himself in *Finnegan's Wake*, though most authors with the talent for punning have tended to suppress that talent, as if it were unsuitable for the purposes of serious art. In the last letter that John Keats is known to have written (it was to Charles Brown, November 30, 1820), he seemed distressed that as his disease began to invade his mental faculties, he was no longer able to restrain his native urge to pun. He wrote that he had "summoned up more puns, in a sort of desperation, in one week than in any year of my life."

It seems clear that the talent for manipulating the sounds and meanings of words automatically carries with it the urge to use the talent. Keats used his to make fine lyric poetry. The gorgeous music of his lines, by the way, probably springs from the same part of his brain as his puns, for both lyricism and clever wordplay require a thorough knowledge and mastery of the ways in which the sounds of the language work. Unlike Keats, Joyce in his writing gave free rein to his genius for punning and showed us that this "lowest form of wit" could be a central ingredient in great art. Not being an artist, my punning friend gave vent to his prowess with words by making linguistic jokes with his friends.

At this point, we may ask a pertinent question: If one is equipped with the ability and urge to exploit the resources of words, what outlets are available to him other than art and essentially harmless wordplay? One outlet, unfortunately, is the irresponsible or dishonest use of elaborate vocabulary that we like to call "propaganda" or sometimes "officialese." If a person is a compulsive whiz at words but lacks moral scruples, and if he doesn't create art or make puns, there is a chance that he will resort to propaganda. During my years in the "humanities," I have seen English professors use words in dishonest ways, both in their tortuously argued critical articles and in their speeches in faculty meetings. A few years ago I heard one of them argue in all seriousness that America is a "police state." Now, it may be true that our country has permitted some serious infringements on our liberties, but it is simply not true that we are, like Nazi Germany or Rome under Tiberius, or the society in *1984*, a "police state." To compare the United States with a police state is legitimate in the fictions of art or in the incongruities of puns or jokes, but in a real and serious context it is dishonest and irresponsible. It is propaganda. It is the kind of thing we might expect from a person who has a need and an ability to exploit the language but has no artistic or comical way to do it.

I don't think that the great books can create, from scratch, the urge to manipulate words. We have to have some of that born in us. However, literature can enlarge the urge and add to it the skills and knowledge necessary to make us into ravagers of the dictionary. And it's fun to be this way. We enjoy the status of being acknowledged by laymen as masters of the language. We have found an easy and lazy way to impress people. Language is exciting too, as the professor who said, "police state" must have sensed. He was very eager and worked-up when he said this, so much so, that one might suspect that he was using the actual issue of injustice as merely a means to use language in what he thought was a dazzling way.

He was like a child who has been given a toy fire truck and is frustrated because there is no fire, or like a child who has received a flashlight and waits impatiently for the dark of night. There seems to be no separating the possession of equipment from the urge to use it.

Section 2

Why We
Write Badly

One night I was up late, reading through a large pile of term papers. These were essays about ten pages long, written by junior and senior English majors taking my eighteenth-century course.

I had placed the main emphasis on Boswell and Johnson and their circle, and a good many of the papers dealt with Johnson as a writer. Some of them pointed out that although he had a powerful mind and a lightning-fast wit, his prose style sometimes left something to be desired. True, there were brilliant sentences such as his epigram on Pope's *Essay on Man:* "Never were penury of knowledge and vulgarity of sentiment so happily disguised." But just as often, the students maintained, you would have to stumble through thickets like this: "The lords might think their dignity diminished by improper advancements, and particularly by the introduction of twelve new peers at once, to produce a majority of Tories in the last reign; an act of authority violent enough, yet certainly legal, and by no means to be compared with that contempt of national right, with which some time afterward, by the instigation of Whiggism, the commons, chosen by the people for three years, chose themselves for seven" *(Life of Addison).* All of the students knew it was bad, and the more discerning ones would point to the unfortunate alliteration of "dignity diminished by improper advancements" and the singsong iambics of "and by no means to be compared with that contempt." The more learned students would comment that Macaulay had a point in his satirical remarks about "Johnsonese."

Because my graduate training had conditioned me to look for "ironies," I noticed that quite a few of the student papers attacking Johnson's style were themselves badly written. Some of them had poor diction—e.g., using "egregious" to mean "excellent" or using nonwords like "levitous" or that old favorite "irregardless." Others had poor sentence structure— e.g., contorted *Time* magazine clauses like "Of great importance in the historicity of English literature was Dr. Johnson." Then I got to thinking about the fact that so many people in the field of literature wrote so badly. It seemed to me that for every author, critic, or student who wrote well, there were at least a dozen bumblers. I came up with the following aphorism: *An activity tends to attract those who are bad at it.* But then I began to realize that my proverb didn't apply to a number of activities which seemed to be well stocked with competent performers: baseball, airline piloting, dentistry, shoe repair, plumbing, accounting, ice hockey, etc. So I had to revise my aphorism to read, *Literature, together with maybe one or two other fields, tends to attract those who are bad at it.*

Having established my principle, I began to look for its ultimate cause. After some reflection, it occurred to me that there are in literature two factors which can make bad writers out of those who read too many novels, poems, or plays. One factor is, quite simply, that most of the literature in existence is badly written. Eighteenth-century England produced literally hundreds of novels, but the first-rate ones like *Robinson Crusoe, Pamela* or *Tom Jones* can be counted on two hands. The odds against producing a classic are dismally overwhelming, and the fact is that most of the literary art in existence is poor. As students and critics of literature, we live each day in an epidemic of failure. It's no wonder that in a short time most of us become inured to it and do so poorly as writers, creating for ourselves a world in which failure or incompetence is not the exception but the norm. We are like a track team that runs the hundred-yard dash in fifteen seconds and feels fine about it.

The second factor that makes us write badly is, conversely, the truly good writing that we find here and there in literature. The excellencies of a major author's style often have the perverse effect of causing us to try to imitate those excellencies, for it's a constant tendency in human nature to ape that which is attractive and well done, and good writing is no exception. However, as Dr. Johnson once wrote (in one of those moments when he had his style under control), "No man was ever great by imitation" *(Rasselas)*. Emerson put it more bluntly: "Imitation is suicide" *(Self-Reliance)*. So insidious is the urge to imitate, that some famous authors have gone down the drain by trying to imitate their own best work and failing in the attempt. Such is the probable reason for the gaucheries of Hemingway's *Across the River and Into the Trees*. But when he went back to being himself, he wrote *The Old Man and the Sea,* a stylistic triumph that helped win its author the Nobel Prize.

More common than the self-imitator is the person who began by imitating an established author. Many major figures in English literature started this way and became great just as soon as they quit imitating. Thus Shakespeare became good when he got off Marlowe, Dryden when he got off Donne, Wordsworth when he got off Thomson, and Thomas when he got off Hopkins. No one denies that imitation is good practice and apprenticeship. The trouble is that too many never progress beyond this initial phase and that those who do go beyond it too often revert back to it. For even with all the originality that we like to attribute to art, art most often has the effect of making copycats out of us. Aristotle said that poetry was imitation, and his disciples (S. H. Butcher, for example) claim that imitation is a creative act. Perhaps it needs to be added that poetry begets a copycat kind of imitation and that this is hardly a creative act.

The problem, then, is that bad literature causes us to lower our standards and that good literature causes us to make poor copies. With this state of affairs, it's no wonder that people who make literary study their career are so frequently inarticulate. Writing too often seems to be an activity which attracts those who are bad at it and keeps them bad or makes them worse. When I think back on the many literature classes I've taught, it occurs to me that often the students who were the best writers were majoring in something else—anthropology, engineering, journalism, physics, pre med, or geography. They seemed to have benefited from their minimal exposure to the great books.

Incidentally, we should ignore English department propaganda that the worst gobbledygook is to be found in the social sciences and education. That's merely a red herring to keep us from noticing the gobbledygook of students and professors in English. I tend to hurl charges without naming names, so I'll pause here to refer you to several well-known works of literary criticism which contain vast sections of the most consummate jargon imaginable: William Empson's *Some Versions of Pastoral*, Rosemond Tuve's *Elizabethan and Metaphysical Imagery*, René Wellek and Austen

Warren's *Theory of Literature*, Geoffrey Hartman's *Beyond Formalism*, and George Willamson's *The Senecan Amble*. The last one, impenetrably written, is a study of English prose style. I haven't meant to imply that these writers are not intelligent; I'm just saying that intelligent people can write badly. I think art helped them do it.

Section 3

Why We Gossip

Rumor is a pipe
Blown by surmises, jealousies, conjectures,
And of so easy and so plain a stop
That the blunt monster with uncounted heads
The still-discordant wavering multitude
Can play upon it.

—*Induction to* King Henry IV, Part II

The word "gossip" derives from a combination of two words, "God" and "sib." "Sib" is related to "sibling," which means "of the same lineage." The derivation of "gossip" implies that all people are related to each other because they are all related to God. A further implication of the word is that because we are all God's creatures, we all have something in common to talk about. It does seem true that gossip is potentially appealing and interesting to any listener. Though its origins are private, it is inherently public. It is exciting because it seems to come to us as an unintentional leak of information.

Another exciting thing about it is that because it is tantalizingly incomplete, it easily fires our imaginations, causing us to add our own fragments and colorings to it before we pass it on. The poet Ambrose Philips put it rather well: "Little gossip, blithe and hale,/ Tattling many a broken tale."

Still another excitement is that gossip makes us feel like insiders. It gives us the illusion that we are an elite few who have been chosen to be let in on the secret. All of us have experienced that titillating feeling when somebody says to us, "Please don't pass this on," "Just between you and me," or "Can you keep a secret?"

We can see from this kind of talk that a further excitement of gossip is

142

that it flatters the ego of the gossiper by giving him an oracular ascendancy over the recipient (he who hears the gossip) and the gossipee (he who is being gossiped about).

Not all people are gossips, but nearly all like to hear gossip. It seems to be true that the more gossip we hear, the more we have the urge to pass it on. It's just too hard to keep bottled up that which seems designed to be shared with everyone. This principle appears to apply equally well to both sexes, and each day there seems to be less evidence to support the old cliché that women are the biggest gossips. Maybe it's the Women's Liberation Movement, or maybe we're beginning to open our eyes and look around. In any event, all sane persons today know that men can be blabbermouths too, even though it's rather difficult for our male egos to admit it.

Some of the largest concentrations of male gossips can be found in organizations like business corporations, branches of government, the armed forces, and universities. The seriousness and intensity of gossip in big institutions ranges all the way from the vicious innuendos of the executive suite to the randy chitchat of the washroom. In the academic world, gossip tends to be petty but nonetheless damaging if it gets to the wrong person. If you keep your ears open around any sizeable university, here is what you might "learn": That the baby of the wife of Professor Green was actually fathered by one of his graduate students. That Professor Brown is having an affair with an undergraduate girl. That Professor Gray is dying of cancer. That Professor Black is going to get fired. That Professor Violet is queer. That Professor Pink is a Communist. That Professor White is a racist. That Professor Blue writes pornography under a pseudonym. And so on, day in and day out.

I have been on college faculties, in the military, in city-government jobs, and in private corporations, and I am convinced that nowhere is gossip so rampant and irresponsible as it is in the academic world. Within this world, the worst gossips of all are in the "humanities." The reason for this is not hard to find. Unlike the rest of the faculty, and unlike those in government or business organizations, people who study and teach art suffer a double exposure to gossip. They are exposed to the rumors and hallway talk that are a normal part of the university environment, but they are also exposed to the gossip that is present in nearly all works of literature.

In a manner of speaking literature is gossip. A good novel, play, or poem often seems to function as an invasion of the privacy of its subject, and the rhetorical effect is to make the reader an eager party to the invasion. A primary purpose of any good creative writer is to take us into private or forbidden areas where we would not normally be allowed to go. To read the great books is to go into Penelope's or Guinevere's royal boudoir at night, an intrusion which theoretically would mean death to all but a privileged few. To read the great books is to learn the nasty secrets of dozens of tragic villains like Medea, Richard the Third, or Faulkner's Jason. It is to learn the contents of Pamela's wardrobe, to hear about the Paris life of Proust's Swann, to watch Babbitt as he gets dressed, and to measure Lolita's bustline. It is to have spilled before you the taboo entrails of hundreds of characters who have dark secrets and dread desires.

Perhaps it can be generalized that the history of literature is marked by a constant shift from mild to more thorough invasions of privacy. The ancient writers intrude into the lady's bedroom; the moderns, into her body. Some very recent works, like *Herzog, Fear Of Flying*, or *Rachel, Rachel*, are nearly one hundred percent invasion of privacy. Books like these score high on the gossip meter, but there is no genuine literary work of art that has a really low reading.

It should be mentioned in passing that a good many writers, in their search for material, end up invading the privacy of real people. Such is almost always the case in satire, which for its material must usually prey upon the supposed vices and follies of actual persons in contemporary life. Thus Aristophanes invaded the privacy of Socrates in *The Clouds*. Horace in his *Satires* pilloried Nasidienus and many others. The angry Juvenal railed at Crispinus. Dante made his enemies writhe in a specially constructed hell. Dryden sneered at the "pigmy body" of the Earl of Shaftesbury. Pope damned Colley Cibber. Byron made the Laureate Southey look incompetent. Lowell saw Poe as "two-fifths sheer fudge." And Malamud in his *A New Life* seems to have skewered the English Department at Oregon State University.

Even in non-satirical writings, the search for material often leads to the real world. Modern Irish writers in particular have a tradition of using actual persons as characters in their works. Examples can be found in Yeats, Joyce, J. M. Synge, and Sean O'Casey. O'Casey went so far as to record the actual conversation of slum dwellers in Dublin and then use it verbatim in his plays, as in the speeches of the drunken Joxer in *Juno and the Paycock*. Some of the playwright's friends felt, justifiably, that they had been betrayed; but his attitude seems to have been that art must prevail, no matter what the price.

It is ironic that although they don't mind disturbing the privacy of others, creative writers are often the first to take offense at anybody else who is a privacy-invader. Shakespeare makes Hamlet become righteously indignant when Rosencrantz, Guildenstern, and Polonius try to "fret" him and "play upon" him; that is, invade his privacy. But the whole play is a symbolic invasion of the privacy of its characters, a beautifully poetic treatment of their innermost feelings and attitudes. A rather constant paradox in literature is the contradiction between the writer's traditional defense of the sanctity of the individual and his meddling in the secrets of the characters he writes about.

Perhaps there is no such thing as a major literary work of art that doesn't go through the motions of invading privacy in some way, for it is the business of the great books to get behind the scenes and lay bare the truth, no matter how bleak, ugly, or embarrassing that truth may be. If there is a hideous skeleton in the closet of Oedipus, it is the duty of art to trot it rattling out into the open. A skillful writer has the ability to make us feel that we have not only an urge but a need and duty to find out every private detail about the characters in his work. When we say that a book caught and held our interest, that it captivated, intrigued, or enthralled us, we mean that it successfully appealed to our sense of gossip and our human tendency to eavesdrop and invade privacy.

It is interesting to note that sometimes the plots of great stories originate in the revealing of an important secret or in the betraying of a precious confidence or trust. When this is the case, the results are often more exciting than the original secret, as in the story of Sisyphus, the mythological character who must forever roll a huge stone uphill. In Book XI of the *Odyssey*, Odysseus says, of his visit to the Underworld, "I saw Sisyphus working at his ceaseless task of pushing his gigantic boulder with both hands. With hands and feet he worked, trying to get it to the hilltop, but always, just before the summit, its weight would overpower him, and the cruel stone would come crashing down again onto the plain. Then he would start over again, sweat running off him and steaming on the ground." Being fascinated with the punishment itself, Homer doesn't bother to tell us what crime Sisyphus committed to deserve this sentence. We have to go elsewhere to find out that his transgression was that he told a secret of Zeus.

Homer's treatment of the myth and his disdain for the actual content of the secret may be used to symbolize a tendency in the great books to look upon privileged information as merely the opportunity for action, drama, and excitement. Many writers throw the emphasis onto the fireworks that come after the initial revelation of the secrets, so that finally the secrets themselves, and the gossips or the tattlers, become relatively unimportant. In the myth of Sisyphus, it is the laboring over the stone that fascinates us, not the fact that Sisyphus couldn't keep a secret. Because authors like Homer focus their powerful artistry on the delicious aftermath of the revelation, they invariably suggest to us that the tattling (or the invading of privacy) really isn't that important. Other famous examples of the Homeric kind of treatment of secrecy are the Prometheus myth and the Adam and Eve story (the "secret" being knowledge of good and evil). In neither of these is the original secret anywhere near as important to the writer and to us as the action and drama that come after it. The effect on us as readers is to lessen our respect for integrity and to increase our contempt for the right to privacy that every individual deserves. We want the action and the drama, and we're willing to pay the price for it.

I have suggested in the foregoing paragraphs that literature can encourage us to be gossips or privacy invaders by (1) stimulating our appetite for gossip or (2) making us willing to sacrifice integrity for excitement. So far we have been looking chiefly at sizeable narrative or dramatic works. What about the lyrical poem? Whose privacy, if anyone's, is invaded here? I think that very frequently the poet invades his own privacy. By making public the inner reaches of his mind and emotions, he eavesdrops on himself. The more intriguingly he gossips about himself, the higher we tend to rate him as a poet. Magnificent self-explorations like *Fern Hill, Sailing to Byzantium, Ode to a Nightingale*, and *Ode on the Intimations of Immortality* owe no small part of their magnificence to the way that they seem to unload secret after secret on the reader. They succeed beautifully in giving us the impression that there is a close and confidential relationship between ourselves and the poet, and that what he tells us about his private self is told in the strictest confidence. But the confidence is designed to be betrayed, and the poet's success is measured by the degree to which we are eager to tell other people his "secrets."

It's not much of an exaggeration to say that to read good lyrical poetry is to be inspired to tattle. The tattling often expands itself beyond the immediate poem to deal with the poem's background and the poet's biography. Thus in speaking of Coleridge, for example, we may speak not only of his poetry but also of his opium problem and his procrastinations. We would gossip about the "gentleman from Porlock," who is supposed to have interrupted the composition of *Kubla Khan*, or about the way that

Wordsworth may have intruded into the last part of the *Ancient Mariner* to tack on a moral: "He prayeth best, who loveth best,/ All things both great and small." Sometimes our gossip about literary backgrounds and biography is lurid, as in our knowledgeable discussions of William Davenant's syphilis, Dr. Johnson's supposed masochistic relationship with Mrs. Thrale, Gibbon's hydrocele, or the homosexuality of Oscar Wilde. It is a favorite teaching device of English professors to lean back in their chairs, cross their legs, and talk matter-of-factly to their students about the seamier sides of writers' lives.

Gossip begets gossip, and it's a natural and easy transition from gossiping about books to gossiping about people. There would be nothing to worry about if the invasion of privacy stopped at the work of art or at the long-deceased artist. Alas, it seldom does. It characteristically spills over into the living world, where it makes two major forms. One is the kind of academic hallway gossip discussed earlier. The other is the literary criticism and scholarship which appears in the learned journals. The articles in these magazines contain a great deal more rhetoric than the scholars writing them are aware of or would willingly acknowledge. The customary rhetorical stance of an author of a piece of scholarship is that he has important inside information on something and that he feels an urgency to pass it on to the next fellow, who he hopes will pass it on to the next fellow after that, and so on. In the course of his article, the scholar, like any other gossip, repeatedly stresses that he has something new and important. Hence the heavy use of such thudding phrases as "this strangely neglected matter," "deserving of further study," "little-known fact," and "heretofore ignored by scholars." Language like this puts us in mind of the truism that it is usually the gossip, and not the gossiper, that is interesting.

From my years of soaking up rumor and hearsay in English departments, I have derived the following principle: generally speaking, the more fascinating the gossip, the duller the gossiper. Perhaps this principle can help to explain why a very interesting novel, poem or play can beget such bland and boring literary criticism and scholarship. On the other hand, we notice that in academic fields in which the subject matter has no entertainment value, the best scholarship often makes lively and absorbing reading. Many of our eminent scientists and social scientists write beautifully. Examples are Linus Pauling, Rachel Carson, David Reisman, and John Kenneth Galbraith.

I think it's fair to conclude that inherent in literature there is something that encourages us to gossip. To live with the great books is to feel a constant pressure to talk about our fellow human beings behind their backs.

Section 4

Does Literature Cause Censorship?

Ne quid res publica detrimenti caperet
(That no harm come to the state)
—*Cicero*, Pro Milone

One day I was thinking about one of Shaw's famous remarks: "Assassination is the extreme form of censorship." I got to wondering if this remark could somehow be applied to John Milton, who had a hand in the beheading of King Charles the First. Was Milton guilty of a kind of censorship when he helped to assassinate the King? (Although Charles was "tried and convicted," his death was really an assassination.) If Milton were guilty of censorship, he might be seen as contradicting his own words. In his *Areopagitica* he had taken a strong stand in favor of freedom of the press. Probably the most famous statement in that treatise is "as good almost kill a man as kill a good book."

To point to the contradictions in a great author's views of censorship is not so much to blame him individually as it is to point to a basic problem in literary art: although literature is always associated with freedom of expression, it seems to have a way of causing censorship. The manner in which literature encourages the suppression of the normal flow of discourse or information can be illustrated by a development that began in Academe about two decades ago. At this time Cliff's Notes and Monarch Notes and their imitators were just beginning to come into popularity. They were very handy. Instead of having to slog through the thousand pages of *Clarissa, An American Tragedy, War and Peace*, or *The*

Magic Mountain, one could buy a set of "notes" for each of these and read the plot summary and critical comments in jig time. The notes were so well done that one could almost always count on getting good grades in literature courses without cracking a book.

Moreover, the notes were usually much cheaper than the actual text. One might have to lay out five or six dollars for a standard edition of *Clarissa*, but the notes could be had for a buck. They were so effective as a short cut that professors as well as students used them. If one were teaching Restoration drama each year, why bother to reread all those tedious plays by Dryden, Etherege, Congreve, and the others, when one could whip through the Monarch outlines in an eighth of the time and still give a respectable lecture? I know of a dozen English professors who regularly lean on the outlines, and every one of these persons has a reputation as a good teacher. A few years ago, one of them received a five hundred dollar award for his outstanding performance in the classroom. I doubt that either faculty or students would have voted him the award if they had had any idea of the degree to which he depended on those slim black and red or striped yellow and black sets of notes. I think the truth was that for years he hadn't reread the stuff he was teaching. It probably bored him to do so.

The trouble with the professor who won the award was not that he used plot summaries but that he was phony about it. He used to condemn them and threaten to flunk any student he caught using them. I don't know if he ever failed anyone for this, but his threats were always delivered in a menacing tone of voice, whether he were lecturing to his class or merely conversing with his colleagues. Perhaps he was more bark than bite, for underneath his formal exterior he really was a gentle person. However, we all would have liked him better if he had been a little less two-faced about the Cliffs and Monarch business. But he persisted in his stance against those "hideous little curbers of intellect," as he called them.

Once, before he discovered their usefulness, he declared that the campus bookstore should stop selling them. Many of his colleagues agreed with him. He said that such "monuments to mindlessness" had no place in "the groves of Academe." I don't know if he ever said anything to the bookstore manager, but even if he had, the manager most likely would have kept right on selling them, for only a few weeks after their introduction they became one of his hottest selling items, and they still are. You can go into any campus bookstore in the country and find specially constructed racks crammed full of Cliffs and Monarch notes on virtually any subject, literary or nonliterary. They have become so thoroughly a part of college life that any effort to ban them from campuses today would not get very far.

And why should anyone want to ban them anyway? After all they are books, and "as good almost kill a man as kill a good book." But are they "good"? I would say yes. In the first place, there is the old but serviceable argument that they're better than nothing. On the other hand, if excessive indulgence in the great books is bad for us, the outlines can furnish us a way to know something about literature and at the same time keep us from being overexposed to it.

In addition, Cliffs or Monarch books are frequently more interesting than the classics they summarize. The Cliffs Notes *Lord Jim* is well written and better any day than the turgid original. The Monarch synopses of eighteenth-century plays are better than eighty percent of the plays summarized. The period in English drama from 1700 to 1800 is commonly acknowledged to be (with a few exceptions like Goldsmith and Sheridan) one of the great wastelands of literature. Yet the Monarch people, God bless them, have succeeded in making it fairly interesting! Then there is the added benefit of providing an opportunity for English professors, who are traditionally underpaid, to make some extra money by writing these summaries. All but a few Cliffs and Monarch outlines are written by college professors, for who is better qualified to do it?

Therefore I have come to the conclusion that Cliffs and Monarch books and their imitators fulfill a useful and noble purpose. Nor does the charge that they "distort" the great books make much sense. A synopsis of a classic is in effect a memory of that classic. No memory of anything is perfect. The act of recall is inevitably an act of distortion, and all we can hope to do is to keep the distortion to a minimum. Most of us would more often trust a printed synopsis memory of a great book than we would trust a lecturing professor's memory of it, especially if, as is too often the case, he hadn't read it for years. And if he were one of those who prepared his classes using Cliffs or Monarch books rather than the real thing, it would be better to trust Cliffs or Monarch rather than his memory of the outlines.

Yet we persist in having guilt feelings about using plot summaries. Professors are still reluctant to admit using them, and students too often shamefacedly hide them under their other books, so that the teacher won't see them. How many of us have wished that whoever designed the cover of the notes had chosen a less garish color scheme? How often have we asked, "Why couldn't they come in discreet black covers or in a disguise as something other than what they are?" To feel guilty about using summaries is to have succumbed to the censorship that is caused by art.

I have talked at length about Cliffs and Monarch books because I feel that they are good illustrations of the fact that literature can cause censorship (1) of itself and (2) of things around it. The great books censor themselves by being sufficiently remote and difficult to scare readers off and to cause them to seek intellectual refuge in the simpler and more accessible contexts of notes, plot outlines, and similar types of aids. If a formidable classic of literary art functions in such a manner as to attract only one or two readers for every ten or twenty that it drives away, it can be said to be censoring itself.

When we turn to look at the way that literature can bring about the censorship of things around it, we point again to the outlines, recalling the efforts of English teachers to keep them out of the classroom, ban them from the campus, or suppress them in some other way. Actions like these are patent acts of censorship, acts which could scarcely occur without the powerful existence of the great books in the first place. There seems to be no escaping the proposition that deep in the nature of art resides some force that militates toward silence, toward hushing our voices in the museum, the library, the painting gallery, and the concert hall.

In the presence of great art, we cannot say anything we want to say. We must be circumspect in our diction, choose our meanings carefully, and argue only the most acceptable of theses. We must be as conservative as the dark stodgy cases in which musical instruments are carried. Then we'll be safe. A graduate student of mine once referred to this situation as "tight assed." What was tight assed, she explained, was the way that people took what she called "the free spirit of art" and turned it into narrow little dogmas of their own concocting, somewhat like in the beginning of *Winesburg, Ohio*. She got upset when I tried to tell her that the dogmas occurred not in spite of art but because of it. She couldn't accept my argument that art, literature in particular, by appearing to be open, loose, indirect, and ambivalent, played upon the contrariness in human nature to inspire people to take the opposite attitude, which was narrowness.

After she went away, I got to reconsidering. Maybe literature was open and loose in its appearances, but wasn't it at the same time a symbolic act of censorship? Wasn't it possible that an author, by the very act of selecting his material, was exercising a kind of censorship? In any case, it occurred to me that no matter how much a writer seemed to tell his audience about his subject, he always held something back, as we could see by studying novels, poems and dramas that made obvious use of "sources." Shakespeare's history plays, for example. These fabulous works may load us up with "information" about English history, but even a glance at Holinshed's Chronicles would show that the playwright omitted a great deal that didn't happen to suit his artistic purposes. Shakespeare censored history, and every writer, whether he draws his "sources" from history, from preexisting fiction, or from his own personal experience, must censor these sources in order to shape his work of art into the unity and coherence which custom demands.

One characteristic of a great work of literature is that it is able to censor its sources while simultaneously giving us the impression that it is telling everything there is to know about those sources—muzzling and revealing at the same time, furnishing at once an excess and a paucity of evidence about its topic. It's different with routine news stories and other types of expository writing. Here the writer is also selective in the use of his sources, but he doesn't try to give the impression that he's not. But we in the "humanities" tend to scorn journalism and devote our full energies to the work of art. Hobnobbing constantly with the subtle selectivity, the careful choosiness, of the great books, we are always in danger of becoming overselective or censorious ourselves.

If it is true, as I've been suggesting, that our classics of literature have the effect not of loosening us up but of restricting us, then we may be justified in looking for possible cause-and-effect relationships between literature and the censorious policies that exist in English departments. The most obvious manifestation of department censorship is the way that professors are penalized for not publishing their articles in the "right" magazines or their books with the "right" university presses. We preach to our students that they mustn't judge a book by its cover; but all too often we turn right around and criticize or condemn our colleagues for appearing in the "wrong" periodicals. Conversely, we tend to assume that anything in a "prestige" journal is good, though such an assumption is nonsense. Yet many a literary scholar has gotten into trouble for publishing in periodicals which the Establishment brands as "light-weight," "secondary," "not scholarly," or "radical."

The academic journals devoted to literature take their place in a definite hierarchy. Serenely at the top is *PMLA* (Publications of the

Modern Language Association). If you can land an article in this organ, you are practically assured of getting tenure and being promoted to associate professor.

Immediately below *PMLA* comes a group of moderately prestigious journals whose titles often contain one or more of the following words: "philology," "studies," "quarterly," "language," or "literature." Examples are *Modern Philology, Studies in Philology, Papers on Language and Literature, Texas Studies in Literature and Language,* and the *New England Quarterly.*

In the third layer from the top of the hierarchy we find a number of good but not classy magazines, whose titles usually don't contain any of the magic words mentioned above. Examples are *College English, Satire Newsletter, Western Humanities Review, Genre,* and *Criticism.*

Toward the bottom of the hierarchy we see a great many periodicals of "dubious reputation." These are the cats and dogs, the fly-by-nighters which define themselves not by being consistently bad but simply by being wildly inconsistent. They print the best and the worst, repeatedly offering their readers gold nuggets mixed with mud, pearls in vinegar; and the unevenness occurs not only among but within the articles. If there is anything consistent about these magazines, it is that in their unpredictable performance they are seldom boring.

There is a group of magazines which lies above and outside of the hierarchy of academic journals headed by *PMLA.* These are the superquality cultural and literary periodicals, including "slicks" like *The New Yorker, Harper's,* and *Atlantic,* and "little magazines" like *Kenyon Review, Sewanee Review,* and *Hudson Review.* In this ethereal realm, one encounters tables of contents that bristle and burn with the brightest names in the literary world. A very honest old professor once told me that he would gladly trade all of his articles in *PMLA* and similar magazines for one appearance in *Sewanee, Kenyon,* or *Hudson.* The difference was, he said, that in the scholarly magazines one gets published by playing the game according to pre-established rules having to do with footnotes, summaries of scholarship, heavy and obvious organization, fanatical accuracy of fact, glittering particularities, and saying the "right" thing, whereas in the high-powered slicks or little magazines one made it on the sheer force of his idea and the artistry with which he presented it.

It occurred to me later that the most original ideas and insights about literature seem to come to us from sources outside the academic world— magazines and presses which aren't attached to universities or which have a great deal of freedom from the schools that subsidize them. I'm thinking of such powerful examples as Susan Sontag's essay "Against Interpretation," Norman Podhoretz's *Making It*, or Morse Peckham's *Man's Rage for Chaos*. These are real breakthroughs, not rehashes of received standard opinion. Sontag's piece appeared in *Evergreen Review*, which is about as far outside Academe as you can get, and Podhoretz's and Peckham's books were printed by nonuniversity presses. But it's an old story: the freshest and most powerful ideas have too often originated outside the academy, coming from nontenured, nonprofessional teachers like Socrates, Confucius, and Christ.

I would say to the English professor who is just starting his career: if you want to make it in the academic world, try to place your articles only in the "acceptable" learned journals, preferably *PMLA* and the ones in the next rank below that. Remember that what counts is not what you publish but where you publish. And remember that if you don't play the game correctly, the old warning of "publish or perish" will turn into the stark eventuality of "publish and perish."

Fledgling assistant professors should also be aware of the *indices expurgatorii* which exist in English departments throughout the land. These are lists of books that you're not supposed to read or even talk about. Unlike the indices of the Catholic Church, English department indices are neither published nor written down. You're supposed to learn them by osmosis. Most of the books on the indices have been put there on the grounds that they're "simplistic," "lightweight," or "popularistic," even though many of them seem to have done people some good. Who are these subversive writers whose words are so vigorously suppressed by English departments? They are none other than such dangerous renegades as Norman Vincent Peale, Dale Carnegie, Billy Graham, and Clifton Fadiman.

Sometimes I wonder if we have made any progress at all since Milton's time. I begin to have my doubts when I see that a large modern English department, which after all exists in the name of language and communication, has a broad stifling policy of censorship. Then I get to thinking that in some ways Milton was more liberal in his censoriousness than we are today. For example, I don't think Milton would ever be guilty of censoring something without reading it first. He might try to censor you or even cut your head off, but before doing so he at least read your stuff and thought about it. He wasn't one of those moderns who merely glances at the covers you appear between, without even bothering to find out what you have to say.

Milton was a muzzler but he was a more honest muzzler than those of today. He took a good stand when he blasted the Catholic church for developing "those catalogues and expurging indexes, that rake through the entrails of many an old good author with a violation worse than any could be offered to his tomb." Those words are from *Areopagitica*. They are the words of a man who had the natural human tendency to censor his fellow men but fought against it. It's a marvel that he was able to liberalize himself as much as he did, living so much of his life in the world of art. Though in many ways he was a contradictory man—humane assassin, woman hating lover, etc.—he was basically a good man, spending most of his career trying to create an atmosphere in which people could say what they really thought and felt. He should be living at this hour.

Index

157

Caedmon, 101
Cambridge History of English Literature, 119
Camus, Albert, 3, 83, 118, 125
Carnegie, Dale, 155
Carroll, Lewis (Charles Lutwidge Dodgson), 54
Carson, Rachel, 147
Castalian Spring, 113
Catastrophe, 66
Catharsis, 66
Catullus, 36, 101
Celestial City, xiii, 97
Cellini, Benvenuto, viii, 73
Cerberus, 119
Cervantes, Miguel de, 52, 67, 92, 100
Charles I, King of England, 147
Chaucer, Geoffrey, 55, 69, 96, 109, 119-20
Chekhov, Anton, 108-9
Chesterfield, Philip Dormer Stanhope, fourth Earl, 112, 113-14
Chicken Little, 103
Chrétien de Troyes, 109
Christ, 32, 47, 58, 71-72, 74, 84, 112, 155
Churchill, Winston, 112
Cibber, Colley, 144
Cicero, 147
Cleopatra, 26
Cliffs Notes, 149 ff.
Coleridge, Samuel Taylor, 79, 84, 89, 146-47
Coles, Robert, 51
College English, 49, 154
Collins, William, 79
Collins, William Wilkie, 6
Collodi, Carlo, 116
Colossus of Memnon, 74
Commentary, 36
Communism, ix, 143
Confucius, 155
Congreve, William, vii, 16, 150
Conrad, Joseph, 24-25, 151
Courtney, W.P., 119
Crabbe, George, 84
Crane, Hart, 36
Crane, Stephen, 20, 100, 124, 125, 130
Crisism, 9, ff.
Crispinus, 144
Criticism, 154
Cyclops (Polyphemus), 44-45

Dante Alighieri, vii, 10, 17, 26, 55, 92, 129, 144
Darlings, professors as, 108 ff.
Darwin, Charles, 42, 128
Davenant, Sir William, 147
Davies, Sir John, 78
Defoe, Daniel, 52, 139
Dickens, Charles, 6, 26, 84, 101
Discus Thrower, 73
Doda, Carole, 134, 135
Donleavy, J.P., 44, 69
Donne, John, 68, 96, 104, 129, 130, 140
Dostoyevsky, Feodor, 53
Drayton, Michael, 35
Dreiser, Theodore, 20, 124, 125, 149
Dryden, John, 36, 134, 140, 144, 150
Dying Gaul, 73

Elgin, Thomas Bruce, seventh Earl, 71, 73
Eliot, George, 2, 6
Eliot, T.S., viii, 10, 84, 86, 89, 96, 119, 125, 129
Emerson, Ralph Waldo, vii, 15, 19, 54, 140
Empson, William, 140
Epic simile, 66
Etherege, Sir George, 150
Eve, 47, 67, 146
Everyman, 84, 109
Existentialism, 3, 83, 109, 118, 121, 125, 128, 130

Fadiman, Clifton, 155
Faulkner, William, 86, 122, 144
Faust, 26
Father of the Bride, 33
Ferrier, Susan Edmonstone, 7
Fichte, Johann Gottlieb, 125
Fielding, Henry, vii, 35, 52, 56, 67, 69, 89-90, 127, 139
Flaubert, Gustave, vii, 25-26, 120-21
Ford, John (seventeenth century), 44
Forster, E.M., 127
Fortune (magazine), 4
Fortune's Wheel, 22
Franklin, Benjamin, 25
Freud, Sigmund, 19, 52, 56, 58, 72, 136
Frost, Robert, 36, 114
Frye, Northrup, 39, 52, 122
Fugitive Group, 110
Fundanius, 32

Langland, William, 22, 63, 109
Laocoön, 73
Laurence, Margaret, 144
Lawrence, D.H., 25, 110
Layamon, 109
Lazarillo de Tormes, 69
Ledwidge, Francis, 30
Leopold, Nathan, 46
Levine, David, 35
Lewis, Sinclair, 67, 144
Lincoln, Abraham, 65
Locke, John, 136
Lope de Vega, 33
Lord Randall, 46
Lovelace, Richard, 36
Lowell, James Russell, 144
Luke, 10, 11, 98, 112
Luther, Martin, 112
Lytton, Edward George Earle Lytton-
Bulwer, first Baron Lytton, 67

M.A. Comprehensive Examination,
51-52, 86
McCarthyism, 12
Macaulay, Thomas Babington, 139
Mackenzie, Henry, 127
Mafia, xi, xii
Malamud, Bernard, 69, 144
Mallarmé, Étienne, 8
Malory, Sir Thomas 84, 109, 129
Malraux, André, 73
Mann, Thomas, 59, 150
Man of the Past, the, 88 ff.
Marcuse, Herbert, viii
Marlowe, Christopher, 10, 44, 68, 100,
140
Marryat, Captain Frederick, 7
Marston, John, 30
Marvel, Andrew, vii, 17, 64, 68
Mary, Virgin, 71-72, 74
Maskell, J., 119
Mather Dynasty (Richard, Increase, Cot-
ton), 80-81, 83
Mayor, J.E.B., 119
Medea, 144
Medusa, viii, 73
Melville, Herman, 26-27, 54
Menander, 17, 32
Meredith, George, 6, 42
Michelangelo (Buonarroti), 71-73
Miller, Arthur, 26
Milton, John, vii, 10, 55, 67, 84, 96,

101, 104, 119, 129, 147, 155
Mitchell, Margaret, 96
Mnemosyne, 113
Modern Language Association, 78
Modern Philology (MP), 11, 154
Molière (Jean Baptiste Poquelin), 33, 52
Monarch Notes, 149 ff.
Montaigne, Michel, vii, 117
Morier, James Justinian, 7
Moses, 72
Mozart, Wolfgang Amadeus, xiii
Muses, 66, 113

Nabokov, Vladimir, 144
Napoleon Bonaparte, 10
Nasidienus, 144
Naturalism, 19 ff., 109, 124-25, 128,
130
Naziism, 47, 48, 91, 137
Nemesis, 30
Nestor, 34
New Comedy, 17, 32-33
New England Quarterly, 154
New Yorker, 154
Nicolas, Sir Harris, 119
Nietzsche, Friedrich Wilhelm, 14
Nixon, Richard M., 35
Norris, Frank, 100, 124
"Now Generation," 2

O'Casey, Sean, 144
Odysseus, 35, 45, 48, 83, 100, 145
Oedipus, viii, 10, 47, 55, 72, 100, 115,
121, 130, 145
Old Comedy, 32-33
Orwell, George, 36, 137
Otway, Thomas, 44
Owen, Wilfred, 30

Paine, Thomas, 9-10
Pandora, 67, 115
Pangloss, 10
Papers on Language and Literature, 154
Paranoia, 81 ff.
Parnassus, 113
Pascal, Blaise, viii
Paul, Saint, 48
Pauling, Linus, 147
Peale, Norman Vincent, 155
Pearl, The (anonymous medieval poem),
109, 119
Peckham, Morse, 155